BF 431 .C2683 199

Calvin, William

How bra

NEW ENGLAND INSTITUTE
OF TECHNOLOGY
LEARNING RESOURCES CENTER

HOW BRAINS THINK

BOOKS BY William H. Calvin

The Cerebral Code
How Brains Think
*Conversations with Neil's Brain**
How the Shaman Stole the Moon
The Ascent of Mind
The Cerebral Symphony
The River That Flows Uphill
The Throwing Madonna
*Inside the Brain**
*with GEORGE A. OJEMANN

HOW BRAINS THINK

Evolving Intelligence, Then and Now

WILLIAM H. CALVIN

 BasicBooks

A Division of HarperCollinsPublishers

NEW ENGLAND INSTITUTE
OF TECHNOLOGY
LEARNING RESOURCES CENTER
35055525
10/96

The Science Masters Series is a global publishing venture consisting of original science books written by leading scientists and published by a worldwide team of twenty-six publishers assembled by John Brockman. The series was conceived by Anthony Cheetham of Orion Publishers and John Brockman of Brockman Inc., a New York literary agency, and developed in coordination with BasicBooks.

• • • • • • • • • • • • • •

The Science Masters name and marks are owned by and licensed to the publisher by Brockman Inc.

• • • • • • • • • • • • • •

Copyright © 1996 by William H. Calvin.
Published by BasicBooks,
A Division of HarperCollins Publishers, Inc.

• • • • • • • • • • • • • •

All rights reserved. Printed in the United States of America. No part of this book may be reproduced in any manner whatsoever without written permission except in the case of brief quotations embodied in critical articles and reviews. For information, address BasicBooks, 10 East 53rd Street, New York, NY 10022–5299.

• • • • • • • • • • • • • •

WCalvin@U.Washington.edu
http://weber.u.washington.edu/~wcalvin

Supplements and corrections to this book can be found at *http://weber.u.washington.edu/~wcalvin/bk8.html*

• • • • • • • • • • • • • •

• • • • • • • • • • • • • •

Library of Congress Cataloging-in-Publication Data
Calvin, William H., 1939–
    How brains think : evolving intelligence, then and now / Willaim H. Calvin.
        p.   cm.
    Includes bibliographical references and index.
    ISBN 0-465-07277-1
    1. Intellect.   2. Human information processing.
3. Brain.   4. Psychology, Comparitive.   I. Title.
    BF431.C2683   1996
    153.9—dc20   96-21086

• • • • • • • • • • • • • •

96 97 98 99 00 ❖/HC 10 9 8 7 6 5 4 3 2

Dedicated to my late futurist friend,
THOMAS F. MANDEL (1946–1995),
whose memes live on.

ACKNOWLEDGMENTS

Helpful discussions with Derek Bickerton, Iain Davidson, Daniel C. Dennett, Stephen Jay Gould, Katherine Graubard (who suggested the book's title), Marcel Kinsbourne, Elizabeth Loftus, Jennifer Lund, Don Michael, George Ojemann, Duane Rumbaugh, Sue Savage-Rumbaugh, Mark Sullivan, and the late Jan Wind are reflected at multiple places in this book. Bonnie Hurren kindly pointed me to the Piagetian definition of intelligence.

The editors at *Scientific American*, John Rennie, Jonathan Piel, and Michelle Press, were very helpful (a short version of my intelligence argument appeared in their "Life in the Universe" special issue of October 1994; well-tuned paragraphs from it are scattered throughout this book), as was Howard Rheingold at *Whole Earth Review* (the last part of the last chapter appeared in their Winter 1993 issue).

Among the others I must thank for their editorial suggestions are Lynn Basa, Hoover Chan, Lena Diethelm, Dan Downs, Seymour Graubard, the late Kathleen Johnston of San Francisco, Fritz Newmeyer, Paolo Pignatelli, Doug vanderHoof, Doug Yanega, and The WELL's writers conference.

Blanche Graubard, as usual, edited the book before it was inflicted on the publisher, and I have again profited from her good sense and style. Jeremiah Lyons and Sara Lippincott edited the book for the Science Masters series and made many excellent suggestions for revision.

CONTENTS

....

It is perfectly true, as philosophers say, that life must be understood backwards. But they forget the other proposition, that it must be lived forwards.

SÖREN KIERKEGAARD, 1843

All organisms with complex nervous systems are faced with the moment-by-moment question that is posed by life: What shall I do next?

SUE SAVAGE-RUMBAUGH and ROGER LEWIN, 1994

Piaget used to say that intelligence is what you use when you don't know what to do (an apt description of my present predicament as I attempt to write about intelligence). If you're good at finding the one right answer to life's multiple-choice questions, you're *smart*. But there's more to being *intelligent*—a creative aspect, whereby you invent something new "on the fly." Indeed, various answers occur to your brain, some better than others.

Every time we contemplate the leftovers in the refrigerator, trying to figure out what else needs to be fetched from the grocery store before fixing dinner, we're exercising an aspect of intelligence not seen in even the smartest ape. The best chefs surprise us with interesting combinations of ingredients, things we would ordinarily never think "went together." Poets are particularly good at arranging words in ways that over-whelm us with intense meaning. Yet we're all constructing brand-new utterances hundreds of times every day, recombin-ing words and gestures to get across a novel message. When-ever you set out to speak a sentence that you've never spoken before, you have the same creativity problem as the chefs and poets—furthermore, you do all your trial and error inside your brain, in the last second before speaking aloud.

We've lately made a lot of progress in locating some aspects of semantics in the brain. Frequently we find verbs in the frontal lobe. Proper names, for some reason, seem to prefer the temporal lobe (its front end; color and tool concepts tend to be found toward the rear of the left temporal lobe). But intelligence is a process, not a place. It's about improvization, where the "sweet spot" is a moving target. It's a way, involv-ing many brain regions, by which we grope for new meanings, often "consciously."

The more experienced writers about intelligence, such as IQ researchers, steer clear of the C word. Many of my fellow neuroscientists avoid consciousness as well (some physicists, alas, have been all too happy to fill the vacuum with begin-ner's mistakes). Some clinicians unintentionally trivialize consciousness by redefining it as mere arousability (though to talk of the brain stem as the seat of consciousness is to thereby confuse the light switch with the light!). Or we redefine con-sciousness as mere awareness, or the "searchlight" of selective attention.

They're all useful lines of inquiry but they leave out that activism of your mental life by which you create—and edit and re-create—yourself. Your intelligent mental life is a fluc-tuating view of your inner and outer worlds. It's partly under your control, partly hidden from your introspection, even capricious (every night, during your four or five episodes of dreaming sleep, it is almost totally out of control). This book tries to fathom how this inner life evolves from one second to the next, as you steer yourself from one topic to another, as you create and reject alternatives. It draws from studies of intelligence by psychologists, but even more from ethology, evolutionary biology, linguistics, and the neurosciences.

THERE USED TO BE SOME GOOD REASONS for avoiding a comprehensive discussion of consciousness and the intellect. A good tactic in science, especially when mechanistic-level explanations don't help structure your approach to a fuzzy subject, is to fragment the problem into bite-sized pieces—and that is, in some sense, what's been going on.

A second reason was to avoid trouble by camouflaging the real issues to all but insiders (maintaining deniability, in the modern idiom). Whenever I see words that have everyday meanings but also far more specific connotations used only by insider groups, I am reminded of code names. Several centuries ago, an uncamouflaged mechanistic analogy to mind could get you into big trouble, even in relatively tolerant Western Europe. Admittedly, Julien Offroy de La Mettrie didn't merely say the wrong thing in casual conversation: this French physician (1709–1751) published a pamphlet in which he wrote of human motivations as if they were analogous to energy-releasing springs inside machines.

That was in 1747; the year before, La Mettrie had fled to Amsterdam from France. He had written a book, it seems, entitled *The Natural History of the Soul*. The Paris Parliament disliked it to the point of ordering all copies burned.

This time, La Mettrie took the precaution of publishing his pamphlet, entitled *Man à Machine*, anonymously. The Dutch, considered the most tolerant people in Europe, were scandalized and tried with a vengeance to discover who the pamphlet's author was. They nearly found out, and so La Mettrie was forced to flee once more—this time to Berlin, where he died four years later, at the age of forty-two.

Though he was clearly ahead of his time, La Mettrie didn't invent the machine metaphor. That's usually ascribed to René Descartes (1596–1650), writing a century earlier, in his *De Homine*. He too had moved to Amsterdam from his native France, at about the same time that Galileo was getting into trouble with the Vatican over the scientific method itself. Descartes didn't have to flee Holland, as did La Mettrie; he took the precaution, one might say, of publishing his book a dozen years after he was safely dead.

Descartes and his followers weren't trying to banish all talk of spirits; indeed, one of their characteristic concerns was to identify exactly where in the brain lay the "seat of the soul." This endeavor was a continuation of a scholastic tradition that focused on the big reservoirs of cerebrospinal fluid inside the brain called the ventricles. Religious scholars of five hundred years ago thought that the subdivisions of the soul were housed in these cavities: memory in one; fantasy, common sense, and imagination in another; rational thought and judgment in a third. Like the bottle with the genie inside, the ventricles were supposedly containers for spirits. Descartes thought that the pineal gland was a better locale for the seat of government, on the grounds that it was one of the few brain structures that didn't come in pairs.

Here at the *fin de millennium,* though there are theocratic countries where using code words would still be a good idea, we are generally more at ease when it comes to machine metaphors for mind. We can even discuss principled grounds for disputing any analogy of mind to machine. Minds, the argument goes, are creative and unpredictable; the machines we know are unimaginative but reliable—so machines such as digital computers initially seem like an unreasonable analogy.

Fair enough. But what Descartes established was that it was useful to talk of the brain *as if* it were a machine. You tend to make progress that way, peeling away the layers of the onion. Even if there is "something else" hidden beneath the obscuring layers, the scientist tentatively assumes that there isn't anything fundamentally *unknowable*, in order to test the alternative explanations. This scientific tactic—not to be confused with a scientific conclusion—has produced a revolution in how we see ourselves.

MECHANISTIC APPROACHES TO MIND were, for a long time, missing an essential ingredient: a bootstrap mechanism. We're used to the idea that a fancy artifact such as a watch requires an even fancier watch designer. It's common sense—just as Aristotle's physics still is (despite being wrong).

But, ever since Darwin, we've known that fancy things can also emerge (indeed, self-organize) from *simpler* beginnings. Even highly educated people, as the philosopher Daniel Dennett notes in the preface to *Darwin's Dangerous Idea*, can be uncomfortable with such bootstrapping notions:

> Darwin's theory of evolution by natural selection has always fascinated me, but over the years I have found a surprising variety of thinkers who cannot conceal their discomfort with his great idea, ranging from nagging skepticism to outright hostility. I have found not just lay people and religious thinkers, but secular philosophers, psychologists, physicists, and even biologists who would prefer, it seems, that Darwin were wrong.

But not all. Only a dozen years after the 1859 publication of *On the Origin of Species*, the psychologist William James was writing letters to friends about his notion that thought involved a darwinian process in the mind. More than a century later, we are only beginning to flesh out this idea with appropriate brain mechanisms for darwinism. For several decades, we have been talking about the selective survival of overproduced synapses. And that's only the cardboard version of darwinism, analogous to carving a pattern into a wood block. Now we're also seeing brain wiring that could operate the full-fledged darwinian process, and probably on the milliseconds-to-minutes timescale of consciousness.

This shaping-up-the-improbable version of darwinism involves generating lots of copies of certain cerebral firing patterns, letting the copies vary somewhat, and then letting those variants compete for dominance over a work space (rather as those variants called bluegrass and crabgrass compete for my backyard). The competition is biased by how well those spatiotemporal firing patterns resonate with the "bumps and ruts in the road"— the memorized patterns stored in the synaptic strengths. Such Darwin Machines are a favorite topic of mine, as you will see, but let us first get some idea of what intelligence is—and isn't.

A USEFUL TACTIC FOR EXPLORING INTELLIGENCE, one that avoids premature definitions, is the journalist's *who-what-where-when-*

why-how checklist. I'll start with *what* constitutes intelligence and *when* intelligence is needed, simply because the term is used in so many ways that it is easy to talk at cross-purposes, just as in the case of consciousness. Narrowing intelligence down a little, without throwing out the baby with the bathwater, is the task of the next chapter, after which I'll tackle levels of explanation and the "consciousness" confusions.

A little ice-age perspective turns out to be important when exploring the evolutionary *why* aspects of intelligence, particularly in discussing our hominid ancestors. Alaska's coastline is the best place to see the ice age still in action; Glacier Bay, some fifty miles long, was totally filled with ice only two hundred years ago. Now it's populated with enough harbor seals, kayaks, and cruise ships to cause traffic jams. In the context of Glacier Bay, I'll raise the question of how jack-of-all-trades abilities could possibly evolve, when efficiency arguments tell us that a streamlined specialist (the lean, mean machine beloved of economists) always does better in any one climate. The short answer? Just keep changing the climate, abruptly and unpredictably, so that efficiency doesn't remain the name of the game.

In the fifth chapter, I'll discuss the mental machinery needed for parsing sentences complicated enough to require syntax. Many observers, myself included, suspect that the big boost in intelligence during hominid evolution was provided by those logical structures needed for a grammatical language (and also useful for other tasks). Chimpanzees and bonobos (these "chimpanzees of the pygmies" are a distinctly different ape, now called by the name that the natives were once said to use) provide some essential perspective for judging the role of language in intelligence and consciousness. Stones and bones are all that's left of our actual ancestors, but our distant cousins show us what ancestral behaviors might have been like.

The sixth chapter takes up the problems of convergent and divergent thinking in the darwinian context. Small neurobiology meetings, such as one I recently attended down on Monterey Bay, certainly illustrate convergent thinking—all those specialists trying to find the one right answer, as the search for memory mechanisms narrows down. But divergent thinking is what creative people need to discover a scientific theory, or write a poem, or (at a more mundane level) dream up all those wrong answers to use in multiple-choice exams for testing convergent thinking. Whenever a neuroscientist proposes an explanation for a memory storage mechanism, questioners from the audience promptly suggest several alternative explanations—ones they've dreamed up on the spot with divergent thinking. So, how do we shape up a novel thought into something of quality, without the equivalent of the guiding hand that shapes up a lump of clay into a pot? The answer may be in the title of chapter 6, "Evolution on-the-Fly." The same darwinian process that shapes up a new species in millennia—or a new antibody during the several weeks of an immune response—may also shape up ideas on the timescale of thought and action.

In the penultimate chapter, I'm going to venture past the analogy of mental processes to other known darwinian processes and propose how (the mechanistic *how* of the physiologist) our brains can manipulate representations in such a way as to cause a copying competition, one that can be darwinian and so shape up randomness into a good guess. This descent into cerebral codes (which, like the bar codes in supermarkets, are abstract patterns that stand in for the real thing) and cerebral circuitry (particularly the circuitry of the superficial cortical layers responsible for the brain's interoffice mail) has provided me with my best glimpse so far of mechanisms for higher intellectual function: how we can guess, speak sentences we've never spoken before, and even operate on a metaphorical plane. It even provides some insight into the big step up from protolanguage to Universal Grammar.

This cerebral version of a Darwin Machine is what, in my opinion, will most fundamentally change our concept of what a person is. Like the Dodo in *Alice in Wonderland*, who said it was better to demonstrate the game than to explain it, I will walk you through the darwinian process in some detail, as it shapes up a thought and makes a decision. Trying to describe intelligence is not, I am happy to report, as difficult as describing how to ride a bicycle; still, you will understand the description a lot better if you develop a feel for the process rather than being satisfied with an abstract appreciation (what you'll get from chapters 6 and 8, if you skip over my favorite chapter).

In the final chapter, I will come back up for air and summarize the crucial elements of higher intelligence described in earlier chapters, focusing on those mechanisms that an exotic or an artificial intelligence would require in order to operate in the range spanning clever chimps to human musical genius. I will conclude with some cautions about any transition to superhuman intelligence, those aspects of arms races that the Red Queen cautioned Alice about—why you have to keep running to stay in the same place.

> *[One doctrine] depicts man as an induction*
> *machine nudged along by external pressures,*
> *and deprived of all initiative and spontaneity.*
> *The second gives him the* Spielraum *[room to*
> *play] to originate ideas and try them out.*
> *Learning about the world means, on the first*
> *view, being conditioned by it; on the second view,*
> *it means adventuring within it.*
>
> J. W. N. WATKINS, 1974

CHAPTER 2

....

EVOLVING A GOOD GUESS

While innate processing, instinctive behavior, internally orchestrated motivation and drive, and innately guided learning are all essential and important elements of an animal's cognitive repertoire, they are not likely to be part of that more esoteric realm of mental activity that we associate with thinking, judgment, and decision making. But what is thought, and how are we to recognize its operation in other creatures within that most private of organs, the brain? What behavioral criteria can permit us to distinguish between the true thought that we are wont to believe goes into our aesthetic, moral, and practical decision making on one hand, and the intricate programming that can create the illusion of thought in at least certain other animals? Or could it be, as advocates of artificial intelligence suspect, that all thought, including ours, is just the consequence of clever programming?

JAMES L. GOULD and CAROL GRANT GOULD,
The Animal Mind, 1994

INTELLIGENCE GETS FRAMED IN SURPRISINGLY NARROW TERMS most of the time, as if it were some more-is-better number that could be assigned to a person in the manner of a batting average. It has always been measured by a varied series of glimpses of spatial abilities, verbal comprehension, word fluency, number facility, inductive reasoning, perceptual speed, deductive reasoning, rote memory, and the like. In recent decades, there has been a tendency to talk about these various subtests as "multiple intelligences." Indeed, why conflate these abilities by trying to boil intelligence down to a single number?

The short answer is that the single number seems to tell us something additional—while hazardous when overgeneralized, it's an interesting bit of information. Here's why: Doing well on one kind of intelligence subtest *never* predicts that you'll do poorly on another; one ability never seems to be at the expense of another. On the other hand, an individual who does well on one such test will often perform better than average on the other subtests.

It's as if there were some common factor at work, such as test-taking ability. The so-called "general factor *g*" expresses this interesting correlation between subtests. The psychologist Arthur Jensen likes to point out that the two strongest influences on *g* are speed (such as how many questions you can answer in a fixed amount of time) and the number of items you can mentally juggle at the same time. Analogy questions (A is to B as C is to [D, E, F]) typically require at least six concepts to be kept in mind simultaneously and compared.

Together, they make high IQ sound like a job description for a high-volume short-order cook, juggling the preparation of six different meals at the same time, hour after hour. Thus, high IQ might be without significance for the kind of lives that most people lead, or important only on those occasions demanding a quick versatility. A high IQ is usually necessary to perform well in very complex or fluid jobs (for example, being a doctor), and it's an advantage in moderately complex ones (secretarial or police work), but it provides little advantage in work that requires only routine, unhurried decision making or simple problem solving (for example, for clerks and cashiers, whose reliability and social skills are likely to be far more important than their IQ).

IQ is certainly one fascinating aspect of intelligence, but it doesn't subsume the others; we shouldn't make the mistake of trying to reduce the subject of *intelligence* to a simple number on a rating scale. That would be like characterizing a football game in terms of one statistic, say, the percent of passes completed. Yes, over the football league as a whole, winning does significantly correlate with that statistic, but there's a lot more to football than just percent-passes-completed; some teams win without completing a single pass, by emphasizing other strengths. IQ does correlate with "winning" in many environments, but it's not what the intelligence game is all about, any more than successful passing is what football is all about.

I think of intelligence as the high-end scenery of neurophysiology—the outcome of many aspects of an individual's brain organization which bear on doing something one has never done before. We may not be able to explain intelligence in all its glory, but we now know some of the elements of an explanation. Some are behavioral, some are neurophysiological, and some are evolutionlike processes that operate in mere seconds. We even know something about the self-organizational principles that lead to emergent stuff—those levels-in-the-making, as when (to anticipate a later chapter) categories and metaphors compete for cerebral territory.

The big issue for understanding intelligence isn't *who* has more but *what* intelligence is, *when* it's needed, and *how* it operates. Some of *what* intelligence encompasses are cleverness, foresight, speed, creativity, and how many things you can juggle at once. More later.

Dɪᴅ ᴏᴜʀ ɪɴᴛᴇʟʟɪɢᴇɴᴄᴇ ᴀʀɪsᴇ from having more of what other animals have? Just looking at the brain and judging it by its size, as if it were a cantaloupe, is apt to be misleading. Only the outer shell, the cerebral cortex, is markedly involved in making novel associations. Most of the brain's bulk comes from the insulation around the "wires" that connect one part of the brain to another; the more insulation, the faster the messages flow. As animals become larger and distances greater, more insulation is needed to speed up transmission and keep the reaction times short; this insulation increases the bulk of the white matter even when the number of cortical neurons stays the same.

An orange peel is only a small part of an orange, and our cerebral cortex is even thinner: about 2 mm, the thickness of two dimes. Our cortex is extensively wrinkled; were it to be peeled off and flattened out, it would cover four sheets of typing paper. A chimpanzee's cortex would fit on one sheet, a monkey's on a postcard, a rat's on a stamp. Were we to mark off a fine grid on the flattened surface, we'd find about the same number of neurons in each little grid square in all cortical regions (except primary visual cortex which, in all binocular animals, has lots of additional small neurons). So if you need more neurons for a particular function, you need more cortical surface area.

We tend to talk of demanding visual tasks for food-finding as "enlarging" monkey visual cortex in later generations but not its auditory cortex, with evolution tending to produce a bulge here—and then, when some other selection pressure comes into play, a bump there. But there is now a strong suspicion that *any* non-olfactory natural selection for more brain space (say vision) results in more brain space for all the other functions as well—that it is often developmentally difficult to make regional enlargements of the brain. So *enlarge one, enlarge them all* may be the general rule, rather than an exception.

And if one evolutionary route to a free lunch isn't enough, here's another: new functions often first appear by making spare-time use of some preexisting part of the brain. Brain regions are, to some extent, multifunctional, resisting our attempts to label them. So, what preexisting functions might be most relevant to the quantum leap in cleverness and foresight during hominid evolution from the apes? Most would say language. I will argue that a "core facility" common to language and to planning hand movements (and used in our spare time for music and dance) has even greater explanatory power than a special facility only for language functions.

INTELLIGENCE IS SOMETIMES DESCRIBED as a patchwork of *know-how* and *know-what* areas in the brain, all those perceptual mechanisms so sensitive to expectations. That is surely true, but if your definition of intelligence is so broad as to include most things that the brain does, such a formulation doesn't advance your understanding any more than extending consciousness to cover plant life does. Catalogs are not explanations, no matter how interesting the list or how much the topics may need inclusion in an introductory course. It's not my purpose to eliminate perceptual mechanisms from intelligence but to illuminate the underpinnings of guessing well and those levels of self-organization that produce stratified stability.

The Spanish physician Juan Huarte defined intelligence in 1575 as the ability to learn, exercise judgment, and be imaginative. In the modern literature, intelligence often connotes the capacity for thinking abstractly, for reasoning, and for organizing large quantities of information into meaningful systems. Not only does this sound like academics trying to define themselves, but it aims too high to be a definition that is readily extended to other animals. A better place to start for the *what* aspects is the animal behavior literature, where good operational definitions of intelligence center on versatility in problem solving.

Bertrand Russell once wryly noted, "Animals studied by Americans rush about frantically, with an incredible display of hustle and pep, and at last achieve the desired result by chance. Animals observed by Germans sit still and think, and at last evolve the solution out of their inner consciousness." Besides being a British commentary on the scientific fashions of 1927, Russell's quip about problem-solving cleverness illustrates the usual false dichotomy between insight and random trial and error. Insight is, beyond argument, intelligent behavior. "Mere randomness" is not, in the usual scheme of things; but we are thereby misled—of which more later.

I like Jean Piaget's emphasis, that intelligence is what you use when you don't know what to do. This captures the element of novelty, the coping and groping ability needed when there is no "right answer," when business as usual isn't likely to suffice. Intelligent improvising. Think of jazz improvisations rather than a highly polished finished product, such as a Mozart or Bach concerto. Intelligence is about the *process* of improvising and polishing on the timescale of thought and action.

The neurobiologist Horace Barlow frames the issue a little

more tightly, and points us toward experimentally testable aspects, by saying that intelligence is all about making a guess—not any old guess, of course, but one that discovers some new underlying order. "Guessing well" neatly covers a lot of ground: finding the solution to a problem or the logic in an argument, happening upon an appropriate analogy, creating a pleasing harmony or a witty reply, correctly predicting what's likely to happen next.

Indeed, you routinely guess what comes next, even subconsciously—say, in listening to a narrative or a melody. Getting a crying child to fill in the last word of each song line is an amazingly effective distraction, seen in many cultures. Subconscious prediction is often why a joke's punch line or a P. D. Q. Bach musical parody brings you up short—you are surprised by the mismatch. Being a little wrong can be amusing, but substantial environmental incoherence is unpleasant, as when a day filled with job insecurity, noise, erratic drivers, and too many strangers leaves you frustrated, because of the frequent mismatch between what you expected and what actually happened.

Calvin's Cure for Environmental Incoherence? Scale back the predictive challenges to a more comfortable level—not all the way into the boredom of surefire predictability but to where you'll be right half the time. That way, you reassure yourself that you're still competent at predicting. Perhaps that's why, after a hard day awash in unpredictability, you tend to seek relief in ritual, music, or sitcoms—anything where you can again take pleasure in frequently guessing what comes next!

ONE OF THE BEGINNER'S ERRORS is to equate intelligence with purpose and complexity. Elaborate, complex behaviors initially seem like a reasonable place to look for signs of intelligence. After all, our language and foresight behaviors are surely aspects of intelligent behavior and they're quite complex.

But many complex behaviors in animals are innate: no learning is needed as they're wired in from birth. Such behaviors tend to be inflexible and often difficult to perform at will, just as sneezing and blushing are. These stereotyped movement patterns exhibit no more insight or understanding of purpose than does a computer program. They're a set piece.

Both innate and learned behaviors can be long and complex. Consider, for example, the performance of an *idiot savant*, a person with enormous detailed recall but poor ability to make good use of the recollected information in a new context, by breaking the pattern into meaningful parts and recombining them. Whale song and insect nest building may be equally unintelligent.

That whales and birds link song sequences together is also not evidence of versatility. The most mindless of behaviors are often linked, the completion of one calling forth the next. Courtship behavior may be followed by intricate nest building, then segue into egg laying, then incubation, then the various stereotyped parental behaviors. Indeed, the more complex and "purposeful" the behavior is, the further it may be from intelligent behavior, simply because natural selection has evolved a surefire way of accomplishing it, with little left to chance. Learning, after all, is usually focused on far simpler things than the complex chains of all-important behaviors.

The animal might understand its own behavior no better than we understand our yawn, or our tendencies to hug and kiss (clearly seen in bonobos and chimpanzees). Most animals in most contexts don't appear to have much need for "understanding"—in our sense of appreciating the underpinnings— and they don't attempt innovations except by modest variations and a slow learning process. It's as if thinking were a little-used backup, too slow and error-prone to be depended on in the normal course of things.

The best indicators of intelligence may be found in the simpler but less predictable problems that confront animals— those rare or novel situations for which evolution has not provided a standard response, so that the animal has to improvise, using its intellectual wherewithal. While we often take "intelligence" to mean both a broad range of abilities and the efficiency with which they're done, it also implies flexibility and creativity—in the words of the ethologists James and Carol Gould, an "ability to slip the bonds of instinct and generate novel solutions to problems." That narrows the *what* field quite a lot.

> *In tests of convergent thinking there is almost
> always one conclusion or answer that is regarded
> as unique, and thinking is to be channeled or
> controlled in the direction of that answer. . . . In
> divergent thinking, on the other hand, there is
> much searching about or going off in various
> directions. This is most obviously seen when
> there are no unique conclusions. Divergent
> thinking . . . is characterized . . . as being less
> goal-bound. There is freedom to go off in
> different directions. . . . Rejecting the old solution
> and striking out in some direction is necessary,
> and the resourceful organism will more probably
> succeed.*
> J. P. GUILFORD, 1959

AREN'T-THEY-CLEVER STORIES are what many people recall when the topic of conversation turns to intelligence. Surely a dog qualifies as intelligent, they will insist. Most such stories turn out to hinge on how well a dog understands English or reads his owner's mind.

Ethologists and animal psychologists will patiently reply that dogs are very social animals, expert in reading body language. A dog is always looking up to his owner, in the same way that a wild dog looks to the pack leader, asking, "What's next, boss?" or emotionally seeking reassurance in a juvenile manner, hoping to elicit benevolence. Talking to domesticated dogs plays into these innate tendencies, though your words per se may not carry the message. People don't realize how much information is conveyed by the tone of voice and body language of the substitute leader (that's you). If you read today's newspaper headline to your dog in the same tone of voice, and with the same glances and postures, as you use to ask him to fetch your slippers, it might work just as well in evoking the desired behavior.

In many cases, there isn't much to confuse the dog. The setting itself (people, places, situations, objects present) provides most of the information the dog needs to respond appropriately to a command. Most dogs have limited repertoires, and it's therefore easy for them to guess correctly. Training a dog to fetch a dozen different items on command is a more difficult proposition, simply because it becomes harder for the dog to guess your intentions.

If you are confident that your dog understands words per se, you might try getting someone else to speak the words from another room over an intercom; this will eliminate most of the situational cues. Many smart animals cannot pass this severe a test of understanding spoken words, not even some extensively tutored chimpanzees who readily respond to graphical symbols. But dogs do pass the lesser test of performing the desired action most of the time, when the situation is familiar and the choices are obvious from the context.

The size of the response repertoire is one important factor in intelligence. Dogs have many instinctive behaviors, such as herding and alarm barks; they can learn many more. Even their communicative repertoire can reach impressive numbers with extensive training, as the psychologist Stanley Coren observes.

> [My pet] dogs have a receptive language of about sixty-five words or phrases and about twenty-five signals or gestures for a total receptive vocabulary of about ninety items. They have a productive language of about twenty-five vocalizations and about thirty-five bodily gestures for a total productive vocabulary of about sixty items. They show no evidence of syntax or grammar. If they were human children, they would be demonstrating the level of language customary at around eighteen to twenty-two months of age. [Bonobos] that have learned [a sign or other symbolic] language can obtain [comprehension] scores equivalent to a child of around thirty months of age.

Speed of learning is also related to intelligence; one reason that dogs and dolphins achieve a wider repertoire of behavior with training is that they learn faster than cats usually do. So, "intelligence" is quite a composite of other things, and many mental abilities are relevant. Perhaps it is making effective combinations of them that better constitutes intelligent behavior.

AN ANIMAL'S SELECTION OF APPROPRIATE BEHAVIOR may be the key to sorting out claims of animal intelligence. In many of the aren't-they-clever animal stories, the animal isn't thinking for itself, but merely responding to a command. Piaget's element of creativity, in the face of an ambiguous task, is usually missing—except during the animal's playful antics.

The scientific literature on nonhuman intelligence tries to cope with innovation, but since most putatively intelligent animal actions are not repeated actions, it's hard to avoid a series of anecdotes (indeed, there's a wonderful book of them about apes, *Machiavellian Intelligence*). The usual scientific hazards of anecdotal evidence can be somewhat reduced by emphasizing comparisons between species. For example, most dogs can't untangle their leashes from around trees, but a chimpanzee seems to have what it takes. A leash-style snap fastener on the door will suffice to keep most small monkeys inside their cage, even if they can reach the fastener to fiddle with it. But the great apes can figure the fastener out, so you must use padlocks—and not leave the key lying around! Chimpanzees can practice deception: a chimp can guess what another animal is likely to be thinking, and can exploit this knowledge. But most monkeys don't seem to have the mental machinery to deceive one another.

To many people, the essence of intelligence is such creative cleverness. When an animal is especially versatile at solving problems or inventing new moves, we consider that behavior to be particularly intelligent. But human intelligence is judged by additional standards.

WHEN I TRIED OUT this "creative cleverness" definition of intelligence on one of my colleagues, he was dubious and started citing examples of the terminally clever.

You know, someone asks you how intelligent a certain person is, and you say, "Well, he's certainly *clever*." By this, you mean that he talks a good line—he's versatile at improvising tactics in the short run but doesn't follow through on his projects and lacks longer-term virtues, such as strategy, perseverance, and good judgment.

OK, I agreed, it also takes foresight to be truly intelligent.

And chimps don't think much about tomorrow, as far as anyone can tell from their behaviors, even if they occasionally do
some planning on the half-hour timescale.

So maybe the flexible future is a human addition to ape
intelligence. Intelligence also involves some imagination, I
continued, remembering a high IQ group for whom I once
gave an after-dinner speech. I had been surprised—in view of
the fact that everyone in the audience had scored high on
intelligence tests—at how unimaginative one of them was,
and then I abruptly realized that I had always thought that IQ
and imagination went hand in hand. But imagination con-
tributes to intelligence only when shaped up into something
of quality.

Patients with hallucinations are pretty imaginative, too,
but that doesn't necessarily make them highly intelligent.

It just goes to show that IQ measures only some aspects of
what we more commonly understand as intelligent behavior.
The very nature of IQ exams tends to preclude tests of creativity or the ability to make plans.

> *If I ever conceive any original idea, it will be
> because I have been abnormally prone to confuse
> ideas . . . and have thus found remote analogies
> and relations which others have not considered!
> Others rarely make these confusions, and
> proceed by precise analysis.*
>
> KENNETH J. W. CRAIK,
> *The Nature of Explanation,* 1943

INNOVATIVE BEHAVIORS are usually not new units; instead, they
are composed of a novel combination of old elements: a
different stimulus evokes a standard behavior, or some new
combination of movements is used in response. How is sen-
sory/movement innovation related to intelligence?

The sheer quantity of building-block types could be important. Cataloging the sensory and movement repertoires, as
Stanley Coren did for dogs, is a useful exercise as long as one
doesn't take the stimulus-response dichotomy too literally.
Sometimes responses appear without apparent triggers; there's
a lot of fiddling around, as when chimps strip the leaves off a

branch for no apparent reason. Often the stimulus-response aspect is muted; the animal will seek out sensations as part of shaping the response. With those cautions, consider some classic examples of stimulus-response.

Many animals have sensory templates, which they try out for size (and shape) on what they see, rather like a child trying out a number of cookie cutters on the baked assortment of Christmas cookies, to see which (if any) fits a particular cookie. Baby birds, for example, crouch when a hawk flies overhead, a behavior suggesting that they were born with the image of a hawk wired into their bird brains. The reality is quite different: initially, they crouch when any sort of bird flies above them. They then come to recognize the sorts of birds they see every day; as a shape becomes familiar, they cease the response to it. Because of such habituation, they eventually crouch only in response to infrequently seen shapes, such as exotic birds that are just passing through— and to predators, such as hawks, which are infrequent because there aren't very many of any species at the top of the food chain.

So the crouch is a response to novelty, not to a pre-wired "alarm" search image. It's as if the child found a misshapen cookie that none of the cookie cutters fitted, and was thereby distressed.

Composers note that while pure overtones (as from the flute) are relatively soothing, random overtones (as in heavy metal or the raspy voices of some singers, such as Mick Jagger) seem to signal threat or alarm, and I've long thought that the disordered sensations produced by nerve injuries are often perceived as painful (rather than merely nonsensical) for the same reason.

Besides sensory templates for familiar sights and sounds, animals also have familiar movement schemas, among which they pick and choose. A cormorant can decide whether to cruise around underwater in search of another meal, or fly away to another pond, or spread its wings to dry (cormorant feathers lack the oil that duck feathers have), or just stand around—presumably by consulting the weightiness of its wings, the fullness of its stomach, its sexual drives, and so forth. Decision making is something that all animals do; it is usually an economistlike weighing of sensations and drives, followed by a standard behavior from its repertoire, as modified by the circumstances.

Of course, we humans often do something similar in deciding on a restaurant, taking into account its menu, parking, cost, travel and waiting time, and ambiance—and somehow comparing all these factors with those of other restaurants. While such weighing of choices seems especially conscious, purposeful, and intentional, choice per se does not imply an extensive mental life—not of the kind we associate with creating novel additions to the list of choices for what to do next ("Suppose there are any *northern* Vietnamese restaurants in town?").

> *Curious, I took a pencil from my pocket and*
> *touched a strand of the [spider] web.*
> *Immediately there was a response. The web,*
> *plucked by its menacing occupant, began to*
> *vibrate until it was a blur. Anything that had*
> *brushed claw or wing against that amazing snare*
> *would be thoroughly entrapped. As the*
> *vibrations slowed, I could see the owner fingering*
> *her guidelines for signs of struggle. A pencil*
> *point was an intrusion into this universe for*
> *which no precedent existed. Spider was*
> *circumscribed by spider ideas; its universe was*
> *spider universe. All outside was irrational,*
> *extraneous, at best raw material for spider. As I*
> *proceeded on my way along the gully, like a vast*
> *impossible shadow, I realized that in the world of*
> *spider I did not exist.*
>
> LOREN EISELEY, *The Star Thrower*, 1978

SOMETIMES AN ANIMAL tries out a new combination of sensory template and movement during play, and finds a use for that combination later on. So perhaps we should add *play* to our list of intelligence attributes.

Many animals, however, are playful only as juveniles. Being an adult is a serious business, with all those mouths to feed, so adults don't have the time or inclination to fool around. A long juvenile period, characteristic of apes and humans, surely aids versatility because of the accumulation of useful combinations. In addition, some evolutionary trends, including domestication of animals, tend to carry over juvenile traits into adulthood—so that, too, might increase versatility.

You don't learn just from your own experiences. You can copy the actions of others, as Japanese monkeys were observed to copy one inventive female's technique for washing the sand off food. You may avoid what seems to spook others, even if you haven't been personally threatened by it, and such "superstitious" behavior can be passed on. The original reason for "Don't step on the crack in the sidewalk" may be lost, but the cultural transmission between generations continues for centuries, sufficient unto itself.

A WIDE REPERTOIRE OF "GOOD MOVES," of course, makes foresight a lot easier. Foresight initially seems simple, almost too simple to be a requirement for high intelligence. But that's because we confuse foresight with species-specific seasonal behaviors.

Squirrels hoarding nuts for winter seems to be the standard example of planning ahead in the animal kingdom. And we now know how such things work. The hormone melatonin, released from the pineal gland during the hours of darkness, serves to warn of the approach of winter. Longer and longer nights result in the release of increasing amounts of melatonin, which in turn triggers food hoarding and new fur coats. It doesn't take much of a brain to do that kind of "planning."

There are, of course, other behaviors created by the brain's initial wiring which serve to set things up for months ahead. Mating behaviors have the effect of producing offspring after a considerable delay. Seasonal migrations come with innate brain wiring or are learned by juveniles and become mindless adult rituals. Of course, such behavior isn't the result of *planning* at all. Seasons are eminently predictable; and over the millennia, plants and animals have been shaped by evolution to sense the signs of approaching winter by means of the innate surefire mechanisms: hoarding nuts probably "feels good" as the days shorten, much as does following the gradient of a sexual pheromone in the air.

Planning on the timescale of a few minutes is seen in some instances, but, as you'll see, none should probably be called *planning.* Keeping a movement plan on hold—as when caged monkeys who have watched food being hidden are able to locate it twenty minutes later, when they are let out of their cages—is sometimes called "planning." But is it simply the memory of an intention? Another disputed type of evidence arises from spatial maneuvering. When bees are kidnapped and carried in a windowless container to a random location several kilometers distant and then released, they quickly set off on the optimal path to an unseen favorite food source. Is this planning, or are they just referencing memories of horizon profiles? Before setting off in the correct direction, they fly a few circles first to get oriented; they may well be scanning the horizon for clues.

Perhaps we should say that *planning* involves something novel, closer to the way in which we procrastinate, figuring out what can safely be put off until tomorrow (or avoided altogether). Indeed, I'd reserve the term for the assembling of multiple stages of the move in advance of action—not when you organize the later stages after getting the initial moves in motion, which goal-plus-feedback can accomplish.

Alas, there is surprisingly little evidence for this kind of multistage planning in the great apes, even in their frequent behaviors. None of the termite-fishing chimps, as the polymath Jacob Bronowski once pointed out, "spends the evening going round and tearing off a nice tidy supply of a dozen probes for tomorrow." Although wild chimps often seem to arrive at a distant fruit tree just as the fruit is ripening, how much of that is migration ritual and how much is all-in-advance planning of a unique route?

For most of your movements, such as raising a coffee cup to your lips, there is time for improvisation en route. If the cup is lighter than you remembered, you can correct its trajectory before it hits your nose. Thus, a complete advance plan really isn't needed; a goal and periodic piecewise elaboration will suffice. You get started in the general direction and then correct your path, just as a moon rocket does. Most "planning" stories involving animals fit into that mold.

Multistage planning is perhaps best seen in an advanced

type of social intelligence: making a mental model of someone else's mental model, then exploiting it. Imagine a chimp that cries "food" in a place where there is no food, and then quietly circles back through the dense forest to where it actually saw the food earlier. While the other chimps beat the bushes at the site of the food cry, the chimp that uttered it gets to eat all the food rather than having to share it.

What's really difficult is to make a detailed advance plan in response to a *unique* situation—like those leftovers in the refrigerator and what might go with them. It requires imagining multiple scenarios, whether you are a hunter plotting various approaches to a deer or a futurist spinning three scenarios bracketing what an industry might look like in another decade. Compared to apes, we do a lot of that: we are even capable of occasionally heeding the eighteenth-century admonition of Edmund Burke, "The public interest requires doing today those things that men of intelligence and goodwill would wish, five or ten years hence, had been done."

So multistage planning for novel situations is surely an aspect of intelligence—indeed, one that appears greatly augmented in the transition from the ape brain to the human brain. But knowledge is, I think, a commonplace.

A BASE OF EXISTING KNOWLEDGE is, of course, required for versatility, foresight, and creativity. You can't be a poet or scientist without a good vocabulary, but definitions of intelligence that stress knowledge or memory's synaptic mechanisms really do miss the mark; they're mistaken reductionism—the practice of reducing something to its fundamental constituents, which for present purposes is carried a few steps too far. This is the mistake, as I explain in the next chapter, that the consciousness physicists often make.

For example, Shakespeare didn't invent the vocabulary he used. He invented combinations of those words, most notably the metaphors that allow relationships to be imported from one level of discourse to another. In a similar manner, much intelligent behavior consists of new combinations of old things.

Deductive logic is another *what* aspect of intelligence—at

least, of the human variety. Philosophers and physicists have, I suspect, been unduly impressed with the human faculty for logical reasoning. Logic might consist of guessing the underlying order of things, à la Horace Barlow, but only in situations where an unambiguous underlying order exists to be guessed (mathematics being the prime exemplar). Piecewise approximation, as with the guessing needed for long division, could operate subconsciously so rapidly as to seem like a leap to the finished "logical" product. Could it be that logic is more a property of the subject matter than of the mental process—that guessing is the name of the game during mental calculations as well as during creative thinking?

The *what* list can be extended further, both for what is and what isn't. But I am going to focus hereafter on Barlow's guessing-at-order aspect and more generally on Piaget's improvisation problem of how to proceed when the choice isn't obvious. I realize that this excludes certain uses of the word "intelligence," as when we talk of intelligent design or military intelligence, but the guessing aspect buys us such a broad range of intelligence connotations that we will do well to organize analysis around it—provided we can avoid consciousness confusions and inappropriate levels of explanation.

> *The mixture of hormone-driven aggression,*
> *sexual and social lust for power, deceit and*
> *gamesmanship, friendship and spite, and good-*
> *and ill-natured fun ring familiar chords. . . .*
> *there is no reasonable way to account for much*
> *of primate (and especially chimpanzee) behavior*
> *without assuming that these animals understand*
> *a great deal about what they are doing and*
> *seeking to do, and are inferring almost as much*
> *as humans do about the intentions and attitudes*
> *of their peers.*
>
> JAMES L. GOULD and CAROL GRANT GOULD,
> *The Animal Mind,* 1994

....

CHAPTER 3

THE JANITOR'S DREAM

*Human consciousness is just about the last
surviving mystery. A mystery is a phenomenon
that people don't know how to think about—yet.
There have been other great mysteries: the
mystery of the origin of the universe, the mystery
of life and reproduction, the mystery of the
design to be found in nature, the mysteries of
time, space, and gravity. These were not just
areas of scientific ignorance, but of utter
bafflement and wonder. We do not yet have all
the answers to any of the questions of cosmology
and particle physics, molecular genetics and
evolutionary theory, but we do know how to
think about them. . . . With consciousness,
however, we are still in a terrible muddle.
Consciousness stands alone today as a topic that
often leaves even the most sophisticated thinkers
tongue-tied and confused. And, as with all of the
earlier mysteries, there are many who insist—
and hope—that there will never be a
demystification of consciousness.*

DANIEL C. DENNETT,
Consciousness Explained, 1991

As CHARLES MINGUS SAID about jazz, you can't improvise from
nothing, you have to improvise from something. The Romans'

phrasing was *Ex nihilo nihil fit.* Creating a novel plan of action has to start somewhere and then refine things. The two greatest examples of creativity in action, species evolution and the immune response, both utilize a darwinian process to shape up crude beginnings into something of quality. But confusions about consciousness (not to mention confusions about levels of mechanisms) usually lead us astray when we attempt to apply darwinism to our mental lives. That's probably why more than a century passed with so little progress on mental darwinism.

In the last chapter, I discussed something of what intelligence is and isn't. Here I am going to attempt the same thing for consciousness, hoping to head off repetitions of those arguments that have sidetracked William James's idea. There is wide overlap between the connotations of consciousness and intelligence, though the C word tends to refer to the waking–aware aspect of our mental lives, while intelligence tends to refer to the imagination or efficiency of our mental lives. Bear in mind that the higher types of intellect may actually require conscious (and therefore subconscious) processing.

HOW SHOULD WE APPROACH explaining the unknown? It is well to keep overall strategy in mind, especially whenever attractive shortcuts are offered as explanations by those whom the philosopher Owen Flanagan terms "the new mysterians." Using Dennett's epigrammatic definition of a mystery, consider for a moment those physicists who are speculating about how quantum mechanics might have a role in consciousness, might provide "free will" an escape route from "determinism" via quantum mechanical processes down at the subcellular level, in the thin microtubules that often cluster near synapses.

I'm not going to take the space needed to do justice to their best-selling arguments (or rather the arguments of their best-selling books), but when you consider how little they actually encompass (let alone explain) of the wide range of themes involved in consciousness and intelligence, you might feel (as I do) that they're just another case of "much ado about very little."

Moreover, as studies of chaos and complexity have been teaching us, determinism is really a nonissue, suitable only for cocktail party conversational gambits and hardly in need of a quantum mechanical escape clause. With some notable exceptions (I call them ecclesiastical neuroscientists, after the great Australian neurophysiologist John C. Eccles), neuroscientists seldom talk in this way; indeed, we rarely engage in any sort of word games about consciousness.

It's not for lack of interest; how the brain works is, after all, our primary preoccupation. Over our beers after a hard day at the neuroscience meetings, we tell each other that while we may not have wide-ranging explanations of consciousness yet, we do know what kinds of explanations don't work. Word games produce more heat than light, and the same is true of explanations that simply replace one mystery with another.

Neuroscientists know that a useful scientific explanation for our inner life has to explain more than just a catalog of mental capabilities. It also has to explain the characteristic errors that the consciousness physicists ignore—the distortions of illusions, the inventiveness of hallucinations, the snares of delusions, the unreliability of memory, and our propensities to mental illnesses and seizures rarely seen in other animals. An explanation has to be consistent with many facts from the last century of brain research—with what we know about consciousness from studies of sleep, strokes, and mental illness. We have numerous ways of ruling out otherwise attractive ideas; I've heard a lot of them in thirty years of doing brain research.

THERE ARE VARIOUS ANGLES along which to cut the cake of our mental lives. I tried focusing on consciousness in *The Cerebral Symphony*. One reason that I'm going to hereafter avoid a discussion of consciousness in favor of intelligence underpinnings is that considerations of consciousness quickly lead to a passive observer as the end point, rather than someone who explores, who adventures within the world. You can see that in the many "consciousness" connotations you'll find in a dictionary:

- Capable of or marked by thought, will, design, or perception.
- Personally felt, as in "conscious guilt."
- Perceiving, apprehending, or noticing, with a degree of controlled thought or observation. (In other words, fully aware.)
- Having mental faculties undulled by sleep, faintness, or stupor: "She became conscious after the anesthesia wore off." (In other words, awake.)
- Done or acting with critical awareness: "He made a conscious effort to avoid the same mistakes." (Here, "deliberate" may substitute for "conscious.")
- Likely to notice, consider, or appraise: "He was a bargain-conscious shopper."
- Marked by concern or interest: "She was a budget-conscious manager."
- Marked by strong feelings or notions: "They are a race-conscious society." (For these last three uses, "sensitive" may be substituted.)

The philosopher Paul M. Churchland has recently made a more useful list, noting that consciousness:

- utilizes short-term memory (or, as it is sometimes called, working memory).
- is independent of sensory inputs, in that we can think about things not present and imagine unreal things.
- displays steerable attention.
- has the capacity for alternative interpretations of complex or ambiguous data.
- disappears in deep sleep.
- reappears in dreaming.
- harbors the contents of several sensory modalities within a single unified experience.

Again, this list has the passive-observer focus rather than the explorer focus, but we see the Piagetian notion of intelligence incorporated into a consciousness definition, in the "alternative interpretations" item.

Among scientists, there is a tendency to use consciousness to mean awareness and recognition; for example, Francis

Crick and Christof Koch use consciousness when addressing the "binding problem" in object recognition and recall. But just because one word (in English) is used to denote these widely different mental faculties doesn't mean that they share the same neural mechanism. Other languages, after all, may assign one or another of the aforementioned "consciousness" connotations its own word. Crick's thalamocortical theory is most useful for thinking about object recognition, but it doesn't say anything about anticipation or decision making— yet those are often among the connotations of consciousness, the word he uses. It's easy to overgeneralize, just by the words you choose. This isn't a criticism: there aren't any good choices until we understand mechanisms better.

By now, the reader might reasonably conclude that consciousness connotations are some sort of intelligence test that examines one's ability to float in ambiguity. Debates about consciousness regularly confuse these connotations with one another, the debaters acting as if they believed in the existence of a common underlying entity—"a little person inside the head"—that sees all. To avoid this presumption of a common mechanism for all connotations, we can use different English words for different connotations, such as when we use "aware" and avoid "conscious." I usually try to do this, but there are also pitfalls when you use alternative words. That's because of what might be termed back-translation.

Physicians, for example, try to avoid the C word by talking instead about the level of arousal that can be achieved with some shouting and prodding of the patient (coma, stupor, alertness, or full orientation to time and place). That's fine, until someone tries to translate back into C-word terminology; yes, a person in a coma is unconscious, but to say that consciousness is at the opposite end of the arousability scale may be seriously misleading.

Worse, equating "conscious" with "arousable" tends to be interpreted as ascribing consciousness to any organism that can experience irritation. Since irritability is a basic property of all living tissue, plant as well as animal, this extends consciousness to almost everything except rocks; some nonscientists are already talking about plant consciousness. While this is appealing to some people and appalling to others, scientifically it is simply bad strategy (even if true). If you throw everything into the consciousness pot and mix it up, you reduce your chances of understanding consciousness.

With so many major synonyms (*aware, sensitive, awake, arousable, deliberate,* and more), you can see why everyone gets a little confused talking about consciousness. One often hears the word's connotation shift in the course of a single discussion; were this to happen to the word "lift," with one speaker meaning what hitchhikers get and the other meaning an elevator, we'd burst out laughing. But when we talk about consciousness, we often fail to notice the shift (and debaters even exploit the ambiguity to score points or sidetrack the argument).

And there's more: at least within the cognitive neuroscience community, consciousness connotations include such aspects of mental life as the focusing of attention, vigilance, mental rehearsal, voluntary actions, subliminal priming, things you didn't know you knew, imagery, understanding, thinking, decision making, altered states of consciousness, and the development of the concept of self in children—all of which grade over into the subconscious as well, all of which have automatic aspects that our "narrator of consciousness" may fail to notice.

Many people think that the narratives we tell ourselves when awake or dreaming tend to structure our consciousness. Narratives are an important part of our sense of self, and not merely in an autobiographical sense. When we play a role— as when the four-year-old engages in make-believe, playing "doctor" or "tea party"— we must temporarily step outside of ourselves, imagine ourselves in someone else's place, and act accordingly. (The ability to do this is one of the more useful definitions of a sense of self.)

But narratives are an automatic part of everyday life in our own skins. Starting around the age of three or four, we make stories out of most things. Syntax is often a junior version of narrative: just the word "lunch" in a sentence sends us looking for variants of the verb "eat," for the food, the place, and persons present. A verb such as "give" sends us searching for the three required nouns we need to fit into roles: an actor, an object given, and a recipient. There are lots of standard relationships, with familiar roles for the players, and we guess from the context what goes into any unfilled gaps. Often we guess well, but dreams illustrate the same kinds of confabulation seen in people with memory disorders, in which bad guesses are unknowingly tolerated.

> *"Perception," it has been recently said, "may be regarded as primarily the modification of an anticipation." It is always an active process, conditioned by our expectations and adapted to situations. Instead of talking of seeing and knowing, we might do a little better to talk of seeing and noticing. We notice only when we look for something, and we look when our attention is aroused by some disequilibrium, a difference between our expectation and the incoming message. We cannot take in all we see in a room, but we notice if something has changed.*
>
> E. M. GOMBRICH, *Art and Illusion*, 1960

A SENSE OF SELF is thought to go along with a fancy mental life, so let me briefly address the common notion that self-awareness (often called self-consciousness) involves sophisticated, "intelligent" mental structures.

How do you know which muscles to move in order to mimic the action of someone else—say, in order to stick out your tongue in response to seeing such an action? Do you have to see yourself in a mirror first, to make the association between that sight and the muscle commands that will mimic it?

No. Newborn humans can imitate some of the facial expressions they see, without any such experience. This suggests that innate wiring connects at least some sensory templates with their corresponding movement commands—that we're "wired to imitate" to some extent. Such wiring might explain why some animals can recognize themselves in a mirror, while others treat their mirror image as another animal, to be coaxed or threatened. Chimps, bonobos, and orangutans can recognize themselves either immediately or within a few days' experience; gorillas, baboons, and most other primates cannot. A capuchin monkey (*Cebus* are the most intelligent of the New World monkeys and the best tool users) with a full-length mirror in its cage may spend weeks threatening the "other animal." Ordinarily, one animal would back down after a brief period, acknowledging the other as dominant. But in the case of the mirror monkey, nothing is ever resolved; even if the capuchin tries acting submissive, so does the other animal. Eventually the monkey begins acting so depressed at the unresolved social conflict that the experimenters must remove the mirror.

What might self-recognition involve? Actions produce expectations about what sensory inflow will result from them (so-called efference copy), and so the perfect fit of these sensory predictions with the inputs from your skin and muscles during small movements would provide a way of recognizing yourself in an image. In the case of wild animals, a perfect fit of the image's movements with internal predictions for facial movements would certainly be unusual, since they rarely see their own face.

The issue of self-consciousness in the animal literature could revolve about something as simple as the attention paid to predictions about facial sensations. That's part of consciousness considerations, certainly, but hardly the pivot that some would make it. Self-recognition surely involves both Horace Barlow's guessing right and Jean Piaget's sophisticated groping, but I'd put it on the list of things that intelligence isn't. Self-recognition is surely more to the point than quantum fields, however.

Do THE ENIGMAS OF QUANTUM MECHANICS really have something to do with such conscious aspects of our mental lives? Or is the invocation of QM in the consciousness context just another mistaken instance of suggesting that one area in which mysterious effects are thought to lurk—chaos, self-organizing automata, fractals, economics, the weather—might be related to another, equally mysterious one? Most such associations certainly conflate the unrelated, and when the two areas are at opposite ends of the spectrum of enigmatic phenomena, the argument is particularly suspicious.

Reducing things to basics— the physicists' rallying cry— is an excellent scientific strategy, as long as the basics are at an appropriate level of organization. In their reductionist enthusiasm, the consciousness physicists act as if they haven't heard of one of the broad characteristics of science: *levels of explanation* (frequently related to *levels of mechanism*). The cognitive scientist Douglas Hofstadter gives a nice example of levels when he points out that the cause of a traffic jam is not to be found within a single car or its elements. Traffic jams are an example of self-organization, more easily recognized when stop-and-go achieves an extreme form of quasi-stability—the crystallization known as gridlock. An occasional traffic jam may be due to component failure, but faulty spark plugs aren't a very illuminating level of analysis—not when compared to merging traffic, comfortable car spacing, driver reaction times, traffic signal settings, and the failure of drivers to accelerate for hills.

The more elementary levels of explanation are largely irrelevant to traffic jams—unless they provide useful analogies. Indeed, packing principles, surface-to-volume ratios, crystallization, chaos, and fractals are seen at multiple levels of organization. That the same principle is seen at several levels does not, however, mean that it constitutes a level-spanning *mechanism:* an analogy does not a mechanism make.

Quasi-stable levels make self-organization easier to spot, especially when building blocks—such as crystals—emerge. Since we are searching for some useful analogies to help explain our mental lives, it is worth examining how levels of explanation have functioned elsewhere. The tumult of random combinations occasionally produces a new form of organization. Some forms, such as the hexagonal cells that appear in the cooking porridge if you forget to stir it, are ephemeral. Other forms may have a "ratchet" that prevents backsliding once some new order is achieved. While crystals are the best known of these quasi-stable forms, molecular conformations are another, and it is even possible that there are quasi-stable forms at intermediate levels—such as microtubule quantum states where the consciousness physicists would like the action to be.

Stratified stability refers to stacking up such quasi-stable levels. Life-forms involve piling up quite a few of them; occasionally they collapse like a house of cards and the higher forms of organization dissolve (which is one way of thinking about death).

Between quantum mechanics and consciousness are perhaps a dozen of these persistent levels of organization: examples include chemical bonds, molecules and their self-organization, molecular biology, genetics, biochemistry, membranes and their ion channels, synapses and their neurotransmitters, the neuron itself, the neural circuit, columns and modules, larger-scale cortical dynamics, and so on. In neuroscience, one is always aware of these levels, because of the intense rivalry between neuroscientists working at adjacent levels.

An occasional alteration in consciousness is due to widespread failures in certain types of synapses. But a more appropriate level of inquiry into consciousness is probably at a level of organization immediately subjacent to that of perception and planning: likely (in my view), cerebral-cortex circuitry and dynamic self-organization involving firing patterns within a constantly shifting quiltwork of postage-stamp-sized cortical regions. Consciousness, in any of its varied connotations, certainly isn't located down in the basement of chemistry or the subbasement of physics. This attempt to leap, in a single bound, from the subbasement of quantum mechanics to the penthouse of consciousness is what I call the Janitor's Dream.

Quantum mechanics is probably essential to consciousness in about the same way as crystals were once essential to radios, or spark plugs are still essential to traffic jams. Necessary, but not sufficient. Interesting in its own right, but a subject related only distantly to our mental lives.

YET, BECAUSE MIND SEEMS "DIFFERENT" FROM MERE MATTER, many people still assume—despite all the foregoing—that this means some spooky stuff is needed to explain it. But the mind should be seen as something like a crystal—comprised of the

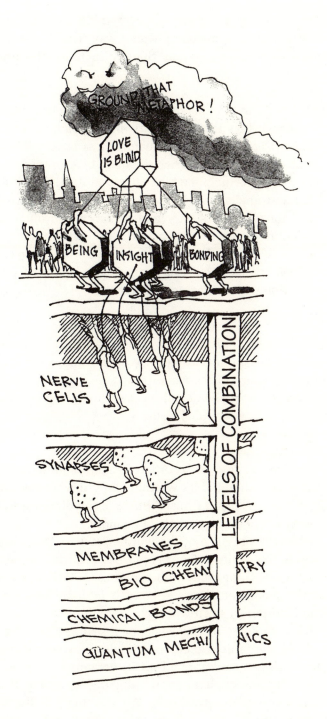

same old matter and energy as everything else, just temporarily organized in some complicated way. This is hardly a new idea; witness Percy Bysshe Shelley in the early nineteenth century:

> It has been the persuasion of an immense majority of human beings that sensibility and thought [as opposed to matter] are, in their own nature, less susceptible of division and decay, and when the body is resolved into its elements, the principle which animated it will remain perpetual and unchanged. However, it is probable that what we call thought is not an actual being, but no more than the relation between certain parts of that infinitely varied mass, of which the rest of the universe is composed, and which ceases to exist as soon as those parts change their position with respect to each other.

The traffic flow patterns in brains are far more complicated than those in vehicular movement; fortunately, there are in music some similarities that we can exploit for analogies. Understanding consciousness and intelligence will require better metaphors and actual mechanisms, not steps backward into word games or spooky stuff.

GHOSTS ARE ANOTHER VERSION OF SPOOKY STUFF, and for our analysis of creative mental life it's worth looking at what has happened to the ghost concept. Ghosts illustrate the other essential creative aspect of mind, the role of memory.

The very presence of the word "ghost" in most languages suggests that quite a few people have needed to talk about inexplicable things they've heard or seen. Why have so many people considered ghosts to be real? Is this where the notion of an incorporeal spirit world got started?

We now know that ghosts appear real because of mistakes made in the brain. Some are trivial, everyday mistakes and others arise from abnormalities in dreaming sleep; a few are stirred up by small epileptic seizures or the pathological processes seen in psychosis. We call them hallucinations; they involve false sounds more often than false sights. The people and pets that they feature are often scrambled a bit, just as they are in the jumble of our nighttime dreams.

Remember that what you see under normal circumstances owes its stability to a mental model that you construct. Your eyes are actually darting all over, producing a retinal image of the scene as jerky as an amateur video, and some of what you thought you saw was instead filled in from memory. In a hallucination, this mental model is carried to an extreme: memories stored inside your brain are interpreted as current sensory input. Sometimes this happens when you are struggling to wake up, when the paralysis of the muscles during dreaming sleep hasn't worn off as fast as usual. Dream elements appear superimposed on the image of real people walking around the bedroom. Or you might hear a dead relative speak to you with a familiar phrase. Half the brain is awake, and the rest is still dreaming away. With any luck, you realize this and don't try to place a more exotic construction on it. Each of us, after all, experiences nightly the symptoms of dementia, delusions, and hallucinations in the course of our dreaming sleep; we're accustomed to discounting such things.

Yet hallucinations can also happen when you are lying awake at night, or when you are working during the day. I suspect that many of these "ghosts" are just simple cognitive mistakes, like one that recently happened to me: I heard a distinct crunching sound in the kitchen, which was repeated a moment later. Ah, I thought as I continued typing, the cat is finally eating her dry food. It took another two seconds before "Oops, let's play that again." The cat, alas, had been dead for several months, and had had a long period of being fussy about her food. What I had faintly heard turned out to be the automatic defroster on our refrigerator—it's somewhat more subtle than the racket made by icemakers—and I had routinely made a guess about what the sound meant without fully considering the matter.

We are always guessing, filling in the details when something is heard faintly. A squeaking screen door, blown by the wind, may sound enough like the I-want-food whine of your dear departed dog for you to "hear" the dog again. Once this memory is recalled, it may be very hard to replay the actual sound you heard—and so the fill-in of details from memory becomes the perceived reality. This isn't unusual; as William James noted a century ago, we do it all the time:

> When we listen to a person speaking or [we] read a page of print, much of what we think we see or hear is supplied from our memory. We overlook misprints, imagining the right letters, though we see the wrong ones; and how little we actually hear, when we listen to speech, we realize when we go to a foreign theatre; for there what troubles us is not so much that we cannot understand what the actors say as that we cannot hear their words. The fact is that we hear quite as little under similar conditions at home, only our mind, being fuller of English verbal associations, supplies the requisite material for comprehension upon a much slighter auditory hint.

This fill-in from memory is part of what's known as *categorical perception*; we just call it a hallucination when we are unaware of what triggered it. Unless a sound repeats, we may not be able to compare our filled-in perception of it to the original; fortunately, where visual phenomena are concerned, we can often manage a second look and catch the mistake before getting committed to "the apparition."

We now know that suggestibility (it doesn't even take hypnosis) and stress (it doesn't even require grieving) can augment our natural tendencies to jump to conclusions, allowing memories to be interpreted as current reality. If I'd been stressed out over something, I might not have searched for an alternative explanation until it was too late to walk into the kitchen and find the sound's true source. Later, upon recalling that I'd "heard" the dead cat, I might have fallen into the common nonscientific explanations: "It was a ghost!" or "I must be losing my mind! Maybe it's Alzheimer's!" Both possibilities are frightening, and both are highly unlikely. But if they're the only explanations that occur to you, you may make yourself quite unhappy.

Have the scientific explanations eliminated ghosts from our culture? At least for those at the educational level of juveniles, the whole notion of ghosts remains a cheap thrill (for exactly the same reason that dinosaurs are so popular with children: they're the potent triple combination of big, scary, and safely dead). Temporal-lobe epileptics, before a physician explains their hallucinations to them, don't think ghosts are funny at all. Grieving relatives may wish, in retrospect, that someone had warned them about meaningless hallucinations.

In this case, science (for those whose education includes it) can eliminate what was once a frightening mystery. Science doesn't merely empower us, as in seeding better technologies; it also helps prevent trouble in the first place. Knowledge can be like a vaccine, immunizing you against false fears and bad moves.

THERE'S A SECOND NEUROSCIENCE GHOST STORY: the philosopher Gilbert Ryle's lovely phrase "the Ghost in the Machine" refers to the little-person-inside manner in which we commonly refer to the "us" inside our brains. It has led some researchers to talk about the "interface" between "mind" and brain, between the unknowable and the knowable. Descartes's pineal gland proposal dressed up in modern clothes by the new mysterians?

We're now making good progress in replacing such pseudo-spirits with better physiological analogies—and even, in some cases, with actual brain mechanisms. Just as an earlier generation of scientists usefully eliminated the external ghosts, I like to think that our currently evolving knowledge about the spirit substitutes will help people think more clearly about themselves and interpret their experiences more reliably, and will help psychiatrists to interpret the symptoms of mental illness.

The consciousness physicists, with their solution in search of a problem, surely aren't intending to tell yet another ghost story. They're just having a good time speculating, in the manner of science fiction writers. (Still, consider how odd it would be for neuroscientists to speculate about the enigmas of physics, even those neurophysiologists—and there are many—who once took several courses in quantum mechanics). But why do these physicists take themselves so seriously, when they're ignoring a dozen levels of organization outside their own specialties? Specialization itself is perhaps part of the answer, and it demonstrates one of the hazards of intelligence.

SPECIALIZATION IN SCIENCE is all about asking answerable questions, which requires focusing on the details—and that takes a lot of time and energy. None of us really wanted to give up those wonderful debates we carried on as undergraduates about the Big Questions. We cared about those questions. They're what attracted us to science in the first place. They're not obsolete, like the ghosts. But the subsequent intellectual development of working scientists sometimes reminds me of what it's it like to be in a canal lock as the water level drops.

At least in Seattle, that's like being in a giant bathtub with a view of waterfront, fish ladders, mountains, and spectators. Once the plug is pulled, your boat sinks, and your attention is captured by the formation of the whirlpools in the lock, which are bouncing the boats about. They're fascinating. If you stick an oar in one, you can spawn off secondary whirlpools. Self-similarity theories suggest themselves, and so begins a digression into fractals.

Should you look up from your experiments and your theorizing in this oversized bathtub, the view of your surroundings will have become a rectangular patch of sky. Now you're looking out from inside a big wet box, whose walls are one or two stories high. In the patch of sunlight on the north wall of the box are some shadows of the people standing topside. As in Plato's Cave, you start to interpret the shadows on the walls, making imperfect guesses about what's really happening up there. What appears to be two people slugging each other turns out to be nothing more than one person standing in front of the other and gesturing wildly while carrying on a conversation.

Specialization can be like that—no more big picture, unless you come up for air occasionally and admire the scenery, see the fuller context.

The price of progress is often an unfamiliarity with other levels of organization, except for those just above or below that of your specialty. (A chemist might know biochemistry and quantum mechanics, but not much neuroanatomy.) When you've got no data but those supplied by your own mental life, it's easy to give fanciful interpretations of the shadows on the wall. Still, sometimes that's the best you can do, and Plato and Descartes did it very well in their day.

But when you can do better, why be satisfied with shadow boxing? Or continue to play word games? A word itself, one eventually realizes, is a very poor approximation of the process it represents. By the end of this book, the reader will, I hope, be able to imagine some neural processes that could result in consciousness—processes that can operate rapidly enough to constitute a quick intelligence.

DESCRIBING OUR MENTAL LIVES has a well-known hang-up, the old subjectivity snare associated with point of view, but there are two other whirlpools we will also need to navigate around.

The passive observer, poised in the mental middle between sensation and action, is a point of view that leads to all sorts of needless philosophical trouble. Partly, that's because sensation is only half of the loop, and we thereby ignore sensation's role in preparing for action. Some of the more elaborate couplings of sensation to action are called "cortical reflexes," but we also need to understand how thought is coupled to action in an intelligent manner, when we grope for a novel course of action. Ignoring the mental middle, as the behavioral psychologists did a half century ago, is not a long-term solution. What neuroscientists often do is investigate the preparation for movement; that gets us closer to the thought process.

We often talk of our mental activities as being subdivided among sensing, thinking, and acting phases. But trouble arises because few things happen at one point in time and space. All of the interesting actions in the brain involve spatiotemporal patterns of cellular activity—not unlike what constitutes a musical melody, where the space is the keyboard or musical scale. All our sensations are patterns spread out in time and space, such as the sensation from your fingers as you get ready to turn to the next page. So too, all our movements are spatiotemporal patterns involving the different muscles and the times at which they are activated. When you turn the page, you are activating about as many muscles as you use in playing the piano (and unless you get the timing just right, you won't be able to separate the next page from the rest). Still, we often try to understand mental events by treating them as if they actually occurred at one place and happened at one instant.

But what's in the mental middle is also a spatiotemporal pattern—the electrical discharges of various neurons—and we shouldn't count on these discharges being funneled through one point in space (such as a particular neuron) and a decision being made at one point in time (such as the moment when that particular neuron discharges an impulse), as if a perception or thought consisted of playing a single note, once. I know of only one such case in vertebrates (occasionally nature makes things convenient for neurophysiologists): it's an escape reflex in fish, conveniently channeled through a single large brain-stem neuron, whose discharge initiates a massive tail flip. But higher functions inevitably involve large overlapping committees of cells, whose actions are spread out in time, and that's a more difficult concept. Understanding higher intellectual function requires us to look at the brain's spatiotemporal patterns, those melodies of the cerebral cortex.

IN ADDITION TO THE NAVIGATIONAL HAZARDS, we need to select our building blocks with care, so that we don't simply replace one mystery with another. Premature closure is the most obvious hazard in selecting building blocks—sometimes we stop surveying candidate mechanisms too early, as when we explain via spirits or quantum fields.

We must also beware of hazards having to do with the end points of an "explanation": the New Age everything-is-related-to-everything and the reductionistic explanations at an inappropriate level of organization (what the consciousness physicists and ecclesiastical neuroscientists do, in my not-so-humble opinion).

Explaining mental life is a big task, and you may have noticed that this is a reasonably thin book. As noted, instead of further exploring consciousness connotations, I'm going to cut the cake differently, focusing on the structures of our mental lives that are associated with intelligence. Intelligence is all about improvising, creating a wide repertoire of behaviors, "good moves" for various situations. A focus on intelligence covers a lot of the same ground as does a focus on consciousness—but it avoids many of the navigational hazards. Most important, the good-moves repertoire is an end point very different from the snapshots of passive contemplation. Certainly it's easier to find a continuity between ourselves and the rest of the animal kingdom by addressing the subject of intelligence, compared to the muddle we generate when we try to talk about animal "consciousness." And so the next task is to take a brief look at where good guessing might have come from, in evolutionary terms.

> *The paradox of consciousness—that the more consciousness one has, the more layers of processing divide one from the world—is, like so much else in nature, a trade-off. Progressive distancing from the external world is simply the price that is paid for knowing anything about the world at all. The deeper and broader [our] consciousness of the world becomes, the more complex the layers of processing necessary to obtain that consciousness.*
>
> DEREK BICKERTON, *Language and Species*, 1990

....

CHAPTER 4

EVOLVING INTELLIGENT ANIMALS

*The apes I know behave every living, breathing
moment as though they have minds that are very
much like my own. They may not think about as
many things, or in the depth that I do, and they
may not plan as far ahead as I do. Apes make
tools and coordinate their actions during the
hunting of prey, such as monkeys. But no ape
has been observed to plan far enough ahead to
combine the skills of tool construction and
hunting for a common purpose. Such activities
were a prime factor in the lives of early
hominids. These greater skills that I have as a
human being are the reason that I am able to
construct my own shelter, earn my own salary,
and follow written laws. They allow me to behave
as a civilized person but they do not mean that I
think while apes merely react.*

SUE SAVAGE-RUMBAUGH, 1994

ANSWERING THE *HOW* QUESTIONS is often our closest approach to
answering a *why* question. Just remember that the answers to
how mechanisms come in two extreme forms, which are
sometimes known as proximate and ultimate causation. Even
the pros sometimes get them mixed up, only to discover that

they've been arguing about two sides of the same coin, so I suspect that a few words of background are needed here.

When you ask, "How does that work?" you sometimes mean *how* in a short-term, mechanical sense—how does something work in one person, right now. But sometimes you mean *how* in a long-term transformational sense—involving a series of animal populations that change during species evolution. The physiological mechanisms underlying intelligent behavior are the proximate *how*; the prehistoric mechanisms that evolved our present brains are the other kind of *how*. You can sometimes "explain" in one sense without even touching upon the other sense of *how*. Such a false sense of completeness is, of course, a good way to get blindsided.

Furthermore, there are different levels of explanation in both cases. Physiological *how* questions can be asked at a number of different levels of organization. Both consciousness and intelligence are at the high end of our mental life, but they are frequently confused with more elementary mental processes—with what we use to recognize a friend or tie a shoelace. Such simpler neural mechanisms are, of course, likely to be the foundations from which our abilities to handle logic and metaphor evolved.

Evolutionary *how* questions also have a number of levels of explanation: just saying that "a mutation did it" isn't likely to be a useful answer to an evolutionary question involving whole populations. Both physiological and evolutionary answers at multiple levels are needed if we are to understand our own intelligence in any detail. They might even help us appreciate how an artificial or an exotic intelligence could evolve—as opposed to creation from top-down design.

EVERYONE WAS ADMIRING THE BALD EAGLES as our cruise ship slipped through the narrow passage at the top end of the Strait of Georgia, between Vancouver Island and the mainland of British Columbia. In one eagle nest after another, busy parents were feeding open mouths.

I was watching the raven, myself. It had found a clam and was trying to break open the shell to get at the innards, which were thus far successfully holding the two halves of the shell tightly together. It picked up the clam in its beak, flew several stories high, and dropped the clam on a rocky area of shoreline. This had to be repeated three times before the raven could settle down to pick his meal out of the shattered shell.

Was that instinctive behavior, or learned by observing others, or learned by trial and accidental success, or intelligently innovative? Did some ancestral raven contemplate the problem and then guess the solution? We have a difficult time seeing the intermediate steps between "reacting" and "thinking," yet we also have an unwarranted faith that "more is better"—that having more behavioral options is better than having fewer.

Nature is full of specialists that do one thing very well, with no frills—like a character actor who only plays one kind of role, never a repertoire. Most animals are specialists. The mountain gorilla, for example, processes fifty monotonous pounds of assorted greenery every single day. The panda's diet is just as specialized.

In terms of finding what they like to eat, neither gorilla nor panda needs to be any smarter than a horse. Their ancestors may have needed to be intelligent in a different niche, but now the gorilla and the panda have each retreated into a niche that doesn't require much intelligence. The same is true of the big-brained marine mammals we saw on the Alaskan cruise— animals that now make their living in more or less the same way as the small-brained fish that specialize in eating other fish.

In comparison, a chimpanzee has a varied diet: fruit, termites, leaves—even meat, when it's lucky enough to catch a small monkey or piglet. So the chimp has to switch around a lot, and that means a lot of mental versatility. But what aids in building up a wide repertoire? One can be born with many movement programs, or learn them, or recombine existing ones in ways that cause novel behaviors to emerge suddenly. Omnivores, such as the octopus, crow, bear, and chimpanzee, have many "moves," simply because their ancestors had to switch among various food sources. Omnivores need a lot more sensory templates too—images and sounds they are in search of.

The other way to accumulate novel behaviors is through social life and play, in both of which new combinations can be discovered. A long life span ought to help both learned and innovative behaviors accumulate, and a long life span is what even the smartest of the invertebrates, the octopus, lacks. (The octopus is about as smart as a rat in some ways.) Smart animals have arisen from various branches of the vertebrate tree of species—ravens among the birds, marine mammals, bears, the primate line.

If specialization is most commonly the name of the game, however, then what selects for versatility? A fickle environment is one answer—an answer that highlights the environmental factor in natural selection. But let me start with another major contributor to sophistication: social life itself, which involves the sexual-selection aspect of natural selection.

SOCIAL INTELLIGENCE is another aspect of intelligence: I refer not to just mimicry but to the challenges that social life (living in groups) poses—challenges that require innovative problem solving. The British psychologist Nicholas Humphrey, for one, considers social interaction, not tool use, to be of primary importance in hominid evolution.

Certainly a social life is an enormous facilitator of an expanded repertoire of actions. Some animals aren't around others of their species long enough to partake of observational learning. Except for brief mating opportunities, adult orang-utans seldom encounter one another, because their food sources are so sparse that it takes a large area to support a single adult. A mother with one offspring is about the biggest social group (except for the transient alliances formed by adolescent orangs), so there's not much opportunity for cultural transmission.

Social life, besides facilitating the spread of new techniques, is also full of interpersonal problems to be solved, like pecking orders. You may need to hide food from the view of the dominant animal, in order to keep it for yourself. You need a lot of sensory templates to avoid confusing one individual with another, and a lot of memory to keep track of your past interactions with each of your colleagues. The challenges

of social life go well beyond the usual environmental challenges to survive and reproduce that the solitary orang con-
fronts. It would therefore seem that a social life is central to
the cultural accumulation of "good moves"—though I suspect
nevertheless that a sociable dog lacks the mental potential of
the solitary orang.

Natural selection for social intelligence may not involve
the usual staying-alive factors commonly stressed in adaptationist arguments. The advantages of social intelligence
would instead manifest themselves primarily via what Darwin called *sexual selection*. Not all adults pass on their
genes. In harem-style mating systems, only a few males get
the chance to mate, after having outsmarted or outpushed the
others. In female-choice mating systems, acceptability as a
social companion is likely to be important for males; for
example, they need to be good at grooming, willing to share
their food, and so forth. The male who can spot approaching
estrus better than other males, and who can persuade the
female to go off into the bushes with him for the duration of
estrus, away from the other males, will stand a much better
chance of passing on his genes, even in a promiscuous mating system. (And this female-choice bootstrap might improve
more than just intelligence: I argue elsewhere that female
choice would have been an excellent setup for improving language abilities, were a female to insist on male language ability at least as good as her own).

> *[S]ocial primates are required by the very nature*
> *of the system they create and maintain to be*
> *calculating beings; they must be able to calculate*
> *the consequences of their own behaviour, to*
> *calculate the likely behaviour of others, to*
> *calculate the balance of advantage and loss—*
> *and all this in a context where the evidence on*
> *which their calculations are based is ephemeral,*
> *ambiguous and liable to change, not the least as*
> *a consequence of their own actions. In such a*
> *situation, "social skill" goes hand in hand with*
> *intellect, and here at last the intellectual*
> *faculties required are of the highest order. The*

game of social plot and counter-plot cannot be
played merely on the basis of accumulated
knowledge. . . . It asks for a level of intelligence
which is, I submit, unparalleled in any other
sphere of living.

NICHOLAS HUMPHREY,
Consciousness Regained, 1984

THE MOST FREQUENT ENVIRONMENTAL STRESS likely to drive natural selection occurs in the temperate zones. Once a year, there is a period of a few months when plants are largely dormant. Eating grass (which stays nutritious even when dormant) is one strategy for getting through the winter. Another, which is much more demanding of versatile neural mechanisms, involves eating animals that eat grass. The extant wild apes all live very close to the equator; while they may have to cope with a dry season, it's nothing like winter's withdrawal of resources.

Climate change is the next most common recurring stress, seen even in the tropics: annual weather patterns shift into a new mode. Multiyear droughts are a familiar example, but sometimes they last for centuries or even millennia. In some cases, there are state-dependent modes of climate. We saw an example in Glacier Bay, just west of Juneau. When explorers passed the mouth of Glacier Bay 200 years ago, they reported that it was full of ice. Now the glaciers have retreated nearly 100 kilometers, and Glacier Bay is open to the sea once more. A series of large glaciers remain in the side valleys, and our ship maneuvered to within a respectful distance of one of these walls of ice; large blocks of it were breaking off and falling into the ocean, even as we watched.

In discussing the local glaciers with a geologist on board, I learned that some were advancing (those are the ones we were taken to see) but that others were in retreat. Advance and retreat at the same time, even in the same valley, and sharing the same climate? What's going on here, I asked?

It's as if a glacier can get stuck in "advance mode" for centuries or millennia, even if the climate cools in the meantime. For example, meltwater from a few hot summers can get underneath and erode the craggy connections to the bedrock, and so the glacier, even if the melting were to stop, can slide downhill faster. That in turn causes the ice to fracture rather than flow when going over bumps, and so more vertical cracks open up. Any meltwater ponds on the surface can then drain down to the bedrock, further greasing the skids and accelerating the movement. The tall mountain of ice starts to collapse by spreading sideways. Eventually you may see glacial surges of the mile-a-month variety—but in Glacier Bay, the ice pushes into the ocean, which erodes it away in giant chunks, that in turn may float away to warmer climates to melt.

Later in the trip we saw Hubbard Glacier, a cliff of ice 5 kilometers long and taller than our ship. Great blocks of ice, loosened by the waves, would periodically crash into the sea. Off to the right side of Yakutat Bay, we could see back up Russell Fjord. Only a decade earlier, the entrance to that fjord was blocked by a surge in Hubbard Glacier. The glacier's advance was faster than the waves could chip it away, so it crept past the mouth of the fjord and dammed it up. Water started rising behind the ice dam, threatening the trapped sea mammals as the salt water became increasingly diluted with the fresh meltwater. When the lake level got up to about two stories above sea level, the ice dam broke.

We know all about glacial surges in Washington State, because they blocked the Columbia River at least 59 times about 13,000 years ago; each time the ice dam broke, a wall of water went racing across the middle of Washington, carving the terrain into scabland as it surged to the sea. (Perhaps the ground-shaking roar warned anyone who was trying to catch salmon in the river valleys to run for the hills.)

Damming up a fjord may have had even more serious consequences. Fjords are often cut off by glacial surges, just as mountain valleys are temporarily dammed by the rubble that avalanches deposit. But dammed-up fjords serve as natural reservoirs for fresh water, and when the ice dam finally breaks, enormous quantities of fresh water flood into the adjacent oceans, a half-year's worth in only a half-day's time. It layers over the ocean surface and only later mixes with the salt water. Unfortunately, that freshening of the surface layer could have major consequences in the case of Greenland's fjords: it is potentially a mechanism for shutting down for a few centuries the North Atlantic Current, which warms Europe—a subject to which I will shortly return.

I tell you all this to point out that there is an enormous asymmetry between the buildup of ice and its subsequent meltdown; this is not at all like the exchange of energy involved in freezing and melting a tray of ice cubes. Buildup mode keeps any cracks filled with new snow and minimizes the greasing of the skids. Melting mode is like a house of cards collapsing in slow motion.

"Modes of operation" are familiar to us from cool-fan-heat modes of air-conditioning systems. Not only do glaciers have modes, but so do ocean currents and continental climates— modes that may be triggered in some cases by glacial surges far away. Sometimes annual temperature and rainfall switch back and forth so rapidly that they have major implications for the evolutionary process, giving versatile animals, like the raven, a real advantage over their lean-mean-machine competitors. That's what this chapter is really about: how the evolutionary crank is turned to yield our kind of versatility— wide repertoires and good guessing get a special kind of boost from a series of climatic instabilities.

PALEOCLIMATOLOGISTS HAVE DISCOVERED that many parts of the earth suffer fairly abrupt climate changes. Decade-long droughts are one example, and we now know something of the thirty-year cycle by which the Sahara expands and contracts. The El Niño cycle, averaging about six years, now appears to have major effects on North American rainfall.

There have also been dozens of episodes in which forests have disappeared over several decades because of drastic drops in temperature and rainfall. In another abrupt change, the warm rains suddenly return a few centuries later— although the last time that Europe reverted to a Siberian-style climate, more than a thousand years passed before it switched back.

In the 1980s, when confirming evidence of these abrupt climate changes was discovered, we thought they were a peculiarity of the ice ages. (Ice sheets have come and gone during the last 2.5 million years, the major meltoffs occurring about every 100,000 years.) None of the abrupt cooling episodes have occurred in the last 10,000 years.

But it turns out that it's only our present interglaciation that has been free of them (so far). The warm times after the last major meltoff, 130,000 years ago, were turbulent in comparison to the present interglaciation; that earlier 10,000-year warm period was punctuated with two abrupt cold episodes. One lasted 70 years, the other 750 years. During them, the German pine forests were replaced with scrubs and herbs now characteristic of central Siberia.

We have thus far been spared such civilization-threatening episodes. Climatically, we have been living in unusually stable times.

A CLIMATE FLIP-FLOP that eliminated fruit trees would be a disaster for regional populations of many monkey species. While it would hurt the more omnivorous as well, they could "make do" with other foods, and their offspring might enjoy a population boom following the crunch, when few competitors would remain.

Such boom times temporarily have enough resources so that most offspring can survive to reproductive age, and this is true even of the odd variants thrown up by the gene shuffles that produce sperm and ova. In ordinary times, such oddities die in childhood, but in a boom time they face little competition; it's as if the usual competitive rules had been suspended temporarily. When the next crunch comes, some odd variants may have better abilities to "make do" with whatever resources are left. The traditional theme extracted from the darwinian process is survival of the fittest, but here we see that it is the *rebound* from hard times that promotes the creative aspects of evolution.

Though Africa was cooling and drying as upright posture was becoming established in hominids about four million years ago, brain size didn't change much. So far, there's not much evidence that brains enlarged during the climate changes in Africa between 3.0 million and 2.6 million years ago—a period in which many new species of African mammals appeared. This isn't the place for an extended discussion of all the factors involved in human evolution, but it is important to note that hominid brain size begins to increase between 2.5 million to 2.0 million years ago and continues for an amazing four-fold expansion in cerebral cortex over the apes. This is the period of the ice ages, and although Africa wasn't a major site of glaciers, the continent probably experienced major fluctuations in climate as the ocean currents rearranged themselves. An ice age is not confined to the Northern Hemisphere; the glaciers in the Andes change at the same time.

The first major episodes of floating ice in the Atlantic occurred at 2.51 million and 2.37 million years ago, with the winter ice pack reaching south to British latitudes. Ice sheets in Antarctica, Greenland, northern Europe, and North America have been with us ever since, melting off occasionally. As noted, we are currently in an interglaciation period, which started about 10,000 years ago. There is a stately rhythm of ice advance and retreat, associated with changes in the earth's axial tilt and its orbit around the sun.

The season of the earth's closest approach to the sun varies; perihelion is currently in the first week of January. Perihelion drifts around the calendar, returning to January in 19,000 to 26,000 years, depending on where the other planets are. The configurations of the other planets approximately repeat about every 400,000 years, though they come close to repeating about every 100,000 years. Their gravitational pull causes the shape of the earth's orbit to vary from near-circular to ellipsoidal. (We're currently about 3 percent farther away from the sun in July, and so receive 7 percent less heat.) Moreover, the tilt of the earth's axis varies between 22.0° and 24.6°, a cycle taking 41,000 years. The last maximum tilt was 9,500 years ago; it's currently 23.4° and declining. The three rhythms combine to contribute to a really major meltoff about every 100,000 years, typically when tilt is maximal and perihelion is also in June; that creates particularly hot summers in the high northern latitudes, where most ice sheets are situated.

Superimposed on the glacial slowness are the aforementioned episodes of abrupt cooling and rewarming. The first one to be discovered happened at a time—13,000 years ago—when all those orbital factors were combining to produce hot

ABRUPT CLIMATE CHANGES DURING THE LAST ICE AGE

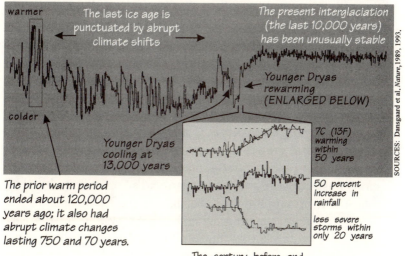

warmer

The last ice age is punctuated by abrupt climate shifts →

The present interglaciation (the last 10,000 years) has been unusually stable

Younger Dryas rewarming (ENLARGED BELOW)

colder

Younger Dryas cooling at 13,000 years

7C (13F) warming within 50 years

50 percent increase in rainfall

less severe storms within only 20 years

The prior warm period ended about 120,000 years ago; it also had abrupt climate changes lasting 750 and 70 years.

SOURCES: Dansgaard et al, *Nature*, 1989, 1993.

The century before and after the abrupt rewarming

summers in the Northern Hemisphere—indeed, half of the accumulated ice had already melted. The Younger Dryas (named for an arctic plant whose pollen was found deep beneath old lakes in Denmark) began quite suddenly. Ice cores from Greenland's ice sheets show that it was as sudden as a drought. Annual rainfall decreased, winter storms grew in severity, and the average European temperature dropped by about 7°C (13°F)—all within several decades. This cold snap lasted more than a thousand years until, just as abruptly, the warm rains returned. (With regard to global warming from greenhouse gases, note that the last time an abrupt cooling happened, it was during a major episode of gradual global warming).

The Greenland ice cores go back only one-tenth of the 2.5 million years of the Pleistocene ice ages; only ice from the last 250,000 years remains in Greenland, because the antepenulti-mate meltoff exposed all the bedrock. But the cores do record the last two major meltoffs—the one that began 130,000 years ago and the most recent one, which began 15,000 years ago and was complete about 8,000 years ago. Most important, one can see annual "tree rings" in the more recent millennia and count the years, sample their oxygen isotopes, and thereby deduce the sea surface temperature at the time the water evaporated in the mid Atlantic before falling as snow in Greenland.

The paleoclimatologists now can see dozens of abrupt events in the last 130,000 years, superimposed upon the glacial slowness—and even occurring during warm periods. Big glacial surges could be one factor—as I discuss in *The Ascent of Mind*—simply because a lot of fresh water floating on the ocean surface before mixing may well cause major changes in the ocean current that imports a lot of heat into the North Atlantic and helps keep Europe warm in the winter. That's why I worry about a glacial surge producing an enormous freshwater reservoir in Greenland's fjords: it could all be released in a day when an ice dam is finally breached. The last time I flew over the extensive fjord system on the east coast of Greenland at 70° north latitude, I was appalled to see fjords that, though open to the ocean, had the bathtub-ring appearance of drawn-down reservoirs. There was an ice-free area extending far above the high-tide line, and everywhere it appeared to be the same height; this suggests an enormous freshwater lake formed sometime since the last ice age, uniformly trimming the ice sheet.

Another cold flip would be devastating to agriculture in Europe, and to the half billion people it supports—and the effects of the Younger Dryas were seen worldwide, even in Australia and Southern California. While another one would threaten civilizations, the cold flips of the past probably played an important role in evolving humans from our apelike ancestors, simply because the episodes happened so rapidly.

> *A round man cannot be expected to fit into a square hole right away. He must have time to modify his shape.*
>
> Mark Twain

WHETHER OR NOT VERSATILITY IS IMPORTANT during an animal's lifespan depends on the timescales: for both the modern traveler and the evolving ape, it's how fast the weather changes and how long the trip lasts. When the chimpanzees of Uganda arrive at a grove of fruit trees, they often discover that the efficient local monkeys are already speedily stripping the trees of edible fruit. The chimps can turn to termite fishing, or perhaps catch a monkey and eat it, but in practice their population is severely limited by that competition, despite the fact that the chimpanzee's brain is twice the size of that of its specialist rivals.

Versatility is not always a virtue, and more of it is not always better. As frequent airline travelers know, passengers who have only carry-on bags can get all the available taxicabs, while those burdened with three suitcases await their checked luggage. On the other hand, if the weather is so unpredictable and extreme that everyone has to travel with clothing ranging from swimsuits to Arctic parkas, the jack-of-all-trades has an advantage over the master of one. And so it is with behavioral versatility that allows a species to switch instantly from round to square holes.

Versatility might well require a bigger brain. But you need some pretty good reasons to balance out the disadvantages of a big brain. As the linguist Steven Pinker has noted:

> Why would evolution ever have selected for sheer bigness of brain, that bulbous, metabolically greedy organ? A large-brained creature is sentenced to a life that combines all the disadvantages of balancing a watermelon on a broomstick . . . and, for women, passing a large kidney stone every few years. Any selection on brain size itself would have surely favored the pinhead. Selection for more powerful computational abilities (language, perception, reasoning, and so on) must have given us a big brain as a by-product, not the other way around!

HOW FAST THINGS CHANGE IS IMPORTANT for any incremental-accumulations model of intelligence, whether it involves a bigger brain or merely a rearranged one. In any one climate, a specialist can eventually evolve that outperforms the overburdened generalist; however, anatomical adaptations occur much more slowly than the frequent climatic changes of the ice ages, making it hard for adaptations to "track" the climate. Indeed, the abrupt transitions can occur within the lifetime of a single individual, who either has the reserve abilities needed to survive the crunch, or doesn't.

This sudden-death-overtime argument applies to many omnivores, not just to our ancestors. But there aren't any other examples around of fourfold brain enlargements in the last several million years, so an erratic climate by itself isn't a surefire way of getting a swelled head. Something else was also going on, and the episodes of abrupt climate change prob- ably exaggerated its importance, and kept those lean-mean- machine competitors from outcompeting the jack-of-all-trades types that evolved.

Everyone has a favorite theory for what this "something else" was. (Nick Humphrey would pick social intelligence as the driver, for example.) My candidate is accurate throwing for hunting—handy for getting through the winter by eating animals that eat grass. But most people would pick language. Especially syntax.

*[Language comprehension] involves many
components of intelligence: recognition of words,
decoding them into meanings, segmenting word
sequences into grammatical constituents,
combining meanings into statements, inferring
connections among statements, holding in short-
term memory earlier concepts while processing
later discourse, inferring the writer's or speaker's
intentions, schematization of the gist of a
passage, and memory retrieval in answering
questions about the passage. . . . [The reader]
constructs a mental representation of the
situation and actions being described. . . .
Readers tend to remember the mental model they
constructed from a text, rather than the text
itself.*
GORDON H. BOWER and DANIEL G. MORROW, 1990

*I often find that a novel, even a well-written and
compelling novel, can become a blur to me soon
after I've finished it. I recollect perfectly the
feeling of reading it, the mood I occupied, but I
am less sure about the narrative details. It is
almost as if the book were, as Wittgenstein said
of his propositions, a ladder to be climbed and
then discarded after it has served its purpose.*
SVEN BIRKERTS, 1994

CHAPTER 5

....

SYNTAX AS A
FOUNDATION OF INTELLIGENCE

*It is hard to imagine how a creature without
language would think, but one may suspect that
a world without any kind of language would in
some ways resemble a world without money—a
world in which actual commodities, rather than
metal or paper symbols for the value of these,
would have to be exchanged. How slow and
cumbersome the simplest sale would be, and
how impossible the more complex ones!*
DEREK BICKERTON, *Language and Species,* 1990

Humans have some spectacular abilities, compared to our
closest cousins among the surviving apes—even the apes that
share much of our social intelligence, reassuring touches, and
abilities to deceive. We have a syntactic language capable of
supporting metaphor and analogical reasoning. We're always
planning ahead, imagining scenarios for the future, and then
choosing in ways that take remote contingencies into account.
We even have music and dance. What were the steps in trans-
forming a chimpanzeelike creature into a nearly human one?
That's a question which is really central to our humanity.

There's no doubt that syntax is what human levels of intelligence are mostly about—that without syntax we would be little cleverer than chimpanzees. The neurologist Oliver Sacks's description of an eleven-year-old deaf boy, reared without sign language for his first ten years, shows what life is like without syntax:

> Joseph saw, distinguished, categorized, used; he had no problems with *perceptual* categorization or generalization, but he could not, it seemed, go much beyond this, hold abstract ideas in mind, reflect, play, plan. He seemed completely literal—unable to juggle images or hypotheses or possibilities, unable to enter an imaginative or figurative realm. . . . He seemed, like an animal, or an infant, to be stuck in the present, to be confined to literal and immediate perception, though made aware of this by a consciousness that no infant could have.

Similar cases also illustrate that any intrinsic aptitude for language must be developed by practice during early childhood. Joseph didn't have the opportunity to observe syntax in operation during his critical years of early childhood: he couldn't hear spoken language, nor he was ever exposed to the syntax of sign language.

There is thought to be a bioprogram, sometimes called Universal Grammar. It is not the mental grammar itself (after all, each dialect has a different one) but rather the predisposition to discover grammars in one's surroundings—indeed, particular grammars, out of a much larger set of possible ones. To understand why humans are so intelligent, we need to understand how our ancestors remodeled the ape's symbolic repertoire and enhanced it by inventing syntax.

STONES AND BONES are, unfortunately, about all that remain of our ancestors in the last four million years, not their higher intellectual abilities. Other species branched off along the way, but they are no longer around to test. We have to go back six million years before there are living species with whom we shared a common ancestor: the nonhominid branch itself split about three million years ago into the chimpanzee and the much rarer bonobo (the "chimpanzee of the Pygmies"). If we want a glimpse at ancestral behaviors, the bonobos are our best chance. They share more behavioral similarities with humans and they're also much better subjects for studying language than the chimps that starred in the sixties and seventies.

Linguists have a bad habit of claiming that anything lacking syntax isn't language. That, ahem, is like saying that a Gregorian chant isn't *music*, merely because it lacks Bach's use of the contrapuntal techniques of stretto, parallel voice leading, and mirror inversions of themes. Since linguistics confines itself to "Bach and beyond," it has primarily fallen to the anthropologists, the ethologists, and the comparative psychologists to be the "musicologists," to grapple with the problem of what came before syntax. The linguists' traditional putdown of all such research ("It isn't really *language*, you know") is a curious category error, since the object of the research is to understand the *antecedents* of the powerful structuring that syntax provides.

One occasionally gets some help from the well-known ontogeny-recapitulates-phylogeny crib, but human language is acquired so rapidly in early childhood that I suspect a streamlining, one that thoroughly obscures any original staging, rather as freeways tend to obliterate post roads. The fast track starts in infants with the development of phoneme boundaries: prototypes become "magnets" that capture variants. Then there's a pronounced acquisitiveness for new words in the second year, for inferring patterns of words in the third (kids suddenly start to use past tense -*ed* and plural -*s* with consistency, a generalization that occurs without a lot of trial and error), and for narratives and fantasy by the fifth. It is fortunate for us that chimps and bonobos lack such fast-tracking, because it gives us a chance to see, in their development, the intermediate stages that were antecedent to our powerful syntax.

VERVET MONKEYS IN THE WILD use four different alarm calls, one for each of their typical predators. They also have other vocalizations to call the group together or to warn of the approach of another group of monkeys. Wild chimpanzees use about three dozen different vocalizations, each of them, like those of the vervets, meaningful in itself. A chimp's loud *waa-bark* is defiant, angry. A soft *cough-bark* is, surprisingly, a threat. *Wraaa* mixes fear with curiosity ("Weird stuff, this!") and the soft *huu* signifies weirdness without hostility ("What *is* this stuff?").

If a *waa-wraaa-huu* is to mean something different than *huu-wraaa-waa*, the chimp would have to suspend judgment, ignoring the standard meanings of each call until the whole string had been received and analyzed. This doesn't happen. Combinations are not used for special meanings.

Humans also have about three dozen units of vocalization, called phonemes—but they're all meaningless! Even most syllables like "ba" and "ga" are meaningless unless combined with other phonemes to make meaningful words, like "bat" or "galaxy." Somewhere along the line, our ancestors stripped most speech sounds of their meaning. Only the combinations of sounds now have meaning: we string together meaningless sounds to make meaningful words. That's not seen anywhere else in the animal kingdom.

Furthermore, there are strings of strings—such as the word phrases that make up this sentence—as if the principle were being repeated on yet another level of organization. Monkeys and apes may repeat an utterance to intensify its meaning (as do many human languages, such as Polynesian), but nonhumans in the wild don't (so far) string together different sounds to create entirely new meanings.

No one has yet explained how our ancestors got over the hump of replacing one-sound/one-meaning with a sequential combinatorial system of meaningless phonemes, but it's probably one of the most important transitions that happened during ape-to-human evolution.

THE HONEYBEE appears, at least in the context of a simple coordinate system, to have broken out of the mold of one-sign/one-meaning. When she returns to her hive, she performs a "waggle dance" in a figure-8 that communicates information about the location of a food source she has just visited. The angle of the figure-8 axis points toward the food.

The duration of the dance is proportional to the distance from the hive: for example, at least in the traditional version of this story, three loops around the figure-8 would suggest 60 meters away to the average Italian honeybee, though 150 meters to a German one—a matter of genes rather than the company in which the bee was reared. Still, the linguists are not very impressed—in his *Language and Species*, Derek Bickerton notes:

> All other creatures can communicate only about things that have evolutionary significance for them, but human beings can communicate about *anything*. . . . Animal calls and signs are structurally holistic [and] cannot be broken down into component parts, as language can. . . . Though in themselves the sounds of [human] language are meaningless, they can be recombined in different ways to yield thousands of words, each distinct in meaning. . . . In just the same way, a finite stock of words . . . can be combined to produce an infinite number of sentences. Nothing remotely like this is found in animal communication.

WITH ENOUGH EXPERIENCE, various animals can learn a wide range of words, symbols, or human gestures—but one must be careful to distinguish between comprehension and the ability to originate fancy communications. They don't necessarily go together.

One psychologist's dog, as I noted earlier, understands about 90 items; the 60 it produces don't overlap very much in meaning with the receptive ones. A sea lion has learned to comprehend 190 human gestures—but it doesn't gesture back with anything near the same productivity. Bonobos have learned an even greater number of symbols for words and can combine them with gestures to make requests. A gray parrot has learned, over the course of a decade, a 70-word vocabulary that includes thirty object names, seven colors, five shape adjectives, and a variety of other "words"—and can make requests with some of them.

None of these talented animals is telling stories about who did what to whom; they're not even discussing the weather. But it is clear that our closest cousins, the chimpanzee and the bonobo, can achieve considerable levels of language *comprehension* with the aid of skilled teachers who can motivate them. The most accomplished bonobo, under the tutelage of Sue Savage-Rumbaugh and her co-workers, can now interpret sentences it has never heard before—such as "Kanzi, go to the office and bring back the red ball"—about as well as a two-and-a-half-year-old child. Neither bonobo nor child is constructing such sentences, but they can demonstrate by their actions that they understand them. And comprehension comes first, production later, as language develops in children.

I often wonder how many of the limited successes in ape language studies were merely a matter of insufficient motivation; perhaps teachers have to be good enough to substitute for the normal self-motivating acquisitiveness of the young child. Or if the limited successes were from not starting with very young animals. If a bonobo could somehow become motivated in its first two years to comprehend new words at a rate approaching that of the year-old child, might the bonobo then go on to discover patterning of words in the manner of the pre-syntax child? But have it happen slowly enough for us to see distinct stages preceding serious syntax, the ones obscured by the streamlined freeways provided by the present human genome?

ALL OF THIS ANIMAL COMMUNICATIVE ABILITY is very impressive, but is it language? The term *language* is used rather loosely by most people. First of all, it refers to a particular dialect such as English, Frisian, and Dutch (and the German of a thousand years ago, from which each was derived—and, further back, proto-Indo-European). But *language* also designates the overarching category of communication systems that are especially elaborate. Bee researchers use *language* to describe what they see their subjects doing, and chimpanzee researchers do the same. At what point do animal symbolic repertoires become humanlike language?

The answer isn't obvious. *Webster's Collegiate Dictionary*

offers "a systematic means of communicating ideas or feelings by use of conventionalized signs, sounds, gestures, or marks having understood meanings" as one definition of *language*. That would encompass the foregoing examples. Sue Savage-Rumbaugh suggests that the essence of *language* is "the ability to tell another individual something he or she did not already know," which, of course, means that the receiving individual is going to have to use some Piagetian guessing-right intelligence in constructing a meaning.

But humanlike language? Linguists will immediately say "No, there are rules!" They will start talking about the rules implied by mental grammar and questioning whether or not these rules are found in any of the nonhuman examples. That some animals such as Kanzi can make use of word order to disambiguate requests does not impress them. The linguist Ray Jackendoff is more diplomatic than most, but has the same bottom line:

> A lot of people have taken the issue to be whether the apes have language or not, citing definitions and counter-definitions to support their position. I think this is a silly dispute, often driven by an interest either in reducing the distance between people and animals or in maintaining this distance at all costs. In an attempt to be less doctrinaire, let's ask: do the apes succeed in *communicating*? Undoubtedly yes. It even looks as if they succeed in communicating *symbolically*, which is pretty impressive. But, going beyond that, it does not look as though they are capable of constructing a mental grammar that regiments the symbols coherently. (Again, a matter of degree—maybe there is a little, but nothing near human capacity.) In short, Universal Grammar, or even something remotely like it, appears to be exclusively human.

What, if anything, does this dispute about True Language have to do with intelligence? Judging by what the linguists have discovered about mental structures and the ape-language researchers have discovered about bonobos inventing rules—quite a lot. Let us start simple.

SOME UTTERANCES ARE SO SIMPLE that fancy rules aren't needed to sort out the elements of the message—most requests such as "banana" and "give" in either sequence get across the message. Simple association suffices. But suppose there are two nouns in a sentence with one verb: how do we associate "dog boy bite" in any order? Not much mental grammar is needed, as boys usually don't bite dogs. But "boy girl touch" is ambiguous without some rule to help you decide which noun is the actor and which is the acted upon.

A simple convention can decide this, such as the subject-verb-object order (SVO) of most declarative sentences in English ("The dog bit the boy") or the SOV of Japanese. In short word phrases, this boils down to the first noun being the actor—a rule that Kanzi probably has absorbed from the way that Savage-Rumbaugh usually phrases requests, such as "Touch the ball to the banana."

You can also tag the words in a phrase in order to designate their role as subject or object, either with conventional inflections or by utilizing special forms called case markings—as when we say "he" to communicate that the person is the subject of the sentence, but "him" when he is the object of the verb or preposition. English once had lots of case markings, such as "ye" for subject and "you" for object, but they now survive mostly in the personal pronouns and in "who"/"whom." Special endings can also tip you off about a word's role in the phrase, as when *-ly* suggests to you that "softly" modifies the verb and not a noun. In highly inflected languages, such markings are extensively used, making word order a minor consideration in identifying the role a word is intended to play in constructing the mental model of relationships.

> *[For] us to be able to speak and understand*
> *novel sentences, we have to store in our heads*
> *not just the words of our language but also the*
> *patterns of sentences possible in our language.*
> *These patterns, in turn, describe not just patterns*
> *of words but also patterns of patterns. Linguists*
> *refer to these patterns as the rules of language*

*stored in memory; they refer to the complete
collection of rules as the mental grammar of the
language, or grammar for short.*
                    RAY JACKENDOFF, *Patterns in the Mind*, 1994

THE SIMPLER WAYS OF GENERATING WORD COLLECTIONS, such as pidgins (or my tourist German), are what the linguist Derek Bickerton calls protolanguage. They don't utilize much in the way of mental rules. The word association ("boy dog bite") carries the message, perhaps with some aid from customary word order such as SVO. Linguists would probably classify the ape language achievements, both comprehension and production, as protolanguage.

Children learn a mental grammar by listening to a language (deaf children by observing sign language). They are acquisitive of associations as well as new words, and one fancy set of associations constitutes the mental grammar of a particular language. Starting at about eighteen months of age, children start to figure out the local rules and eventually begin using them in their own sentences. They may not be able to describe the parts of speech, or diagram a sentence, but their "language machine" seems to know all about such matters after a year's experience.

This biological tendency to discover and imitate order is so strong that deaf playmates may invent their own sign language ("home sign") with inflections, if they aren't properly exposed to one they can model. Bickerton showed that the children of immigrants invent a new language—a creole—out of the pidgin protolanguage they hear their parents speaking. A pidgin is what traders, tourists, and "guest workers" (and, in the old days, slaves) use to communicate when they don't share a real language. There's usually a lot of gesturing, and it takes a long time to say a little, because of all those circumlocutions.

In a proper language with lots of rules (that mental grammar), you can pack a lot of meaning into a short sentence. Creoles are indeed proper languages: the children of pidgin speakers take the vocabulary they hear and create some rules for it—a mental grammar. The rules aren't necessarily any of those they know from simultaneously learning their parents' native languages. And so a new language emerges, from the mouths of children, as they quickly describe who did what to whom.

WHICH ASPECTS OF LANGUAGE ARE EASY to acquire and which are difficult? Broad categories may be the easiest, as when the child goes through a phase of designating any four-legged animal as "doggie" or any adult male as "Daddy." Going from the general to the specific is more difficult. But some animals, as we have seen, can eventually learn hundreds of symbolic representations.

A more important issue may be whether new categories can be created that escape old ones. The comparative psychologist Duane Rumbaugh notes that prosimians (lorises, galagos, and so forth) and small monkeys often get trapped by the first set of discrimination rules they are taught, unlike rhesus monkeys and apes, both of which can learn a new set of rules that violates the old one. We too can overlay a new category atop an old one, but it is sometimes difficult: categorical perception (the pigeonholing mentioned earlier, in association with auditory hallucinations) is why some Japanese have such a hard time distinguishing between the English sounds for L and R.

The Japanese language has an intermediate phoneme, a neighbor to both L and R. Those English phonemes are, mistakenly, treated as mere variants on the Japanese phoneme. Because of this "capture" by the traditional category, those Japanese speakers who can't hear the difference will also have trouble pronouncing them distinctly.

Combining a word with a gesture is somewhat more sophisticated than one-word, one-meaning—and putting a few words together into a string of unique meaning is considerably more difficult. Basic word order is helpful in resolving ambiguities, as when you can't otherwise tell which noun is the actor and which the acted upon. The SVO declarative sentence of English is only one of the six permutations of those units, and each permutation is found in some human language. Some word orders are more frequently found than others, but the variety suggests that word order is a cultural convention rather than a biological imperative in the manner proposed for Universal Grammar.

Words to indicate points in time ("tomorrow" or "before") require more advanced abilities, as do words that indicate a desire for information ("What" or "Are there") and the words for possibility ("might" or "could"). It is worthwhile noting what a pidgin protolanguage lacks: it doesn't use articles like "a" or "the," which help you know whether a noun refers to a particular object or simply the general class of objects. It doesn't use inflections (-s, -ly, and the like) or subordinate clauses, and it often omits the verb, which is guessed from the context.

Though they take time to learn, vocabulary and basic word order are nonetheless easier than the other rule-bound parts of language. Indeed, in the studies of Jacqueline S. Johnson and Elissa L. Newport, Asian immigrants who learn English as adults succeed with vocabulary and basic word-order sentences, but have great difficulty with other tasks—tasks that those who arrived as children easily master. At least in English, the who-what-where-when-why-how questions deviate from basic word order: "What did John give to Betty?" is the usual convention (except on quiz shows in which questions mimic the basic word order and use emphasis instead: "John gave *what* to Betty?"). Nonbasic word orders in English are difficult for those who immigrated as adults, and so are other long-range dependencies, such as when plural object names must match plural verbs, despite many intervening adjectives. Not only do adult immigrants commit such grammatical errors, but they can't detect errors when they hear them. For example, the inflectional system of English alters a noun when it refers to a multiplicity ("The boy ate three cookie." Is that normal English?) and alters a verb when it refers to past time ("Yesterday the girl pet a dog." OK?). Those who arrived in the United States before the age of seven make few such recognition errors as adults, and there is a steady rise in error rate for adults who began learning English between the ages of seven and fifteen—at which age the adult error level is reached (I should emphasize that the linguists were, in all cases, testing immigrants with ten years' exposure to English, who score normally on vocabulary and the interpretation of basic word-order sentences).

By the age of two or three, children learn the plural rule: add -s. Before that, they treat all nouns as irregular. But even if they had been saying "mice," once they learn the plural rule they may begin saying "mouses" instead. Eventually they learn to treat the irregular nouns and verbs as special cases, exceptions to the rules. Not only are children becoming acquisitive of the regular rules at about the time of their second birthday but it also appears that the window of opportunity is closing during the school years. It may not be impossible to learn such things as an adult, but simple immersion in an English-language society does not work for adults in the way that it does for children aged two to seven.

Whether you want to call it a bioprogram or a Universal Grammar, learning the hardest aspects of language seems to be made easier by a childhood acquisitiveness that has a biological basis, just as does learning to walk upright. Perhaps this acquisitiveness is specific to language, perhaps it merely looks for intricate patterns in sound and sight and learns to mimic them. A deaf child like Joseph who regularly watched chess games might, for all we know, discover chess patterns instead. In many ways, this pattern-seeking bioprogram looks like an important underpinning for human levels of intelligence.

A DICTIONARY WILL DEFINE THE WORD *GRAMMAR* for you as (1) morphology (word forms and endings); (2) syntax (from the Greek "to arrange together"—the ordering of words into clauses and sentences); and (3) phonology (speech sounds and their arrangements). But just as we often use *grammar* loosely to refer to socially correct usage, the linguists sometimes go to the opposite extreme, using overly narrow rather than overly broad definitions. They often use *grammar* to specify just a piece of the mental grammar—all the little helper words, like "near," "above," and "into," that aid in communicating such information as relative position. Whatever words like these are called, they too are quite important for our analysis of intelligence.

First of all, such grammatical items can express relative location (*above, below, in, on, at, by, next to*) and relative direction (*to, from, through, left, right, up, down*). Then there are the words for relative time (*before, after, while,* and the various indicators of tense) and relative number (*many, few, some,* the *-s* of plurality). The articles express a presumed familiarity or unfamiliarity (*the* for things the speaker thinks the hearer will recognize, *a* or *an* for things the speaker thinks the hearer won't recognize) in a manner somewhat like pronouns. Other grammatical items in Bickerton's list express relative possibility (*can, may, might*), relative contingency (*unless, although, until, because*), possession (*of,* the possessive version of *-s, have*), agency (*by*), purpose (*for*), necessity (*must, have to*), obligation (*should, ought to*), existence (*be*), nonexistence (*no, none, not, un-*), and so on. Some languages have verbal inflections that indicate whether you know something on the basis of personal experience or just at second hand.

So grammatical words help to position objects and events relative to each other on a mental map of relationships. Because relationships ("bigger," "faster," and so forth) are what analogies usually compare (as in "bigger-is-faster"), this positioning-words aspect of grammar could also augment intelligence.

SYNTAX IS A TREELIKE STRUCTURING of relative relationships in your mental model of things which goes far beyond conventional word order or the aforementioned "positioning" aspects of grammar. By means of syntax, a speaker can quickly convey a mental model to a listener of who did what to whom. These relationships are best represented by an upside-down tree structure—not the sentence diagraming of my high school days, but a modern version of diagraming known as an X-bar phrase structure. Since there are now some excellent popular books on this subject, I will omit explaining the diagrams here *(whew!)*.

Treelike structure is most obvious when you consider subordinate clauses, as in the rhyme about the house that Jack built. ("This is the farmer sowing the corn/ That kept the cock that crowed in the morn/ . . . That lay in the house that Jack built.") Bickerton explains that such nesting or embedding is possible because

> phrases are not, as they might appear to be, strung together serially, like beads on a string. Phrases are like Chinese boxes, stacked inside one another. The importance of this point can hardly be overestimated. Many people concerned with the origins of human language, or with the alleged language capacities of non-human species, have been led to propose grossly simplistic hypotheses about how language could have emerged, simply on the basis of a mistaken assumption. They assume that words are serially chained into phrases and phrases into sentences in pretty much the same way that steps are chained into walking. . . . Nothing could be further from the truth. . . . This can be seen by considering a phrase like *the cow with the crumpled horn that Farmer Giles likes.* Although no single word in this phrase is ambiguous, the phrase as a whole is, because we do not know whether it is the horn or the cow that Farmer Giles likes.

In addition to such "phrase structure" (as this is called), there is "argument structure," which is particularly helpful in guessing the role of the various nouns in the sentence. If you see an intransitive verb, such as "sleep," you can be sure that one noun (or pronoun) will suffice to complete the thought— namely, the actor. This will be true in any language with a word for sleeping. Similarly, if a language has a verb meaning "beat," you can be sure that two nouns are involved, an actor and a recipient (and perhaps a third, for the instrument with which the beating is administered). A verb meaning "give" calls for three nouns, as it also requires an item that is given to the recipient. So, any mental organization chart featuring "give" will have three empty slots, which must be appropriately filled before you feel that you correctly "understand" the sentence and can proceed to the next task. Sometimes the nouns are implicit, as in the exhortation "Give!" where we fill in "you," "money," and "to me" automatically.

As Bickerton notes, a sentence is like

a little play or story, one in which each of the characters has a specific role to perform. There is a finite and indeed very short list of these roles. Not all linguists are agreed as to exactly what they are, but most, if not all, would include the roles of Agent (*JOHN cooked dinner*), Patient or Theme (*John cooked DINNER*), Goal (*I gave it TO MARY*), Source (*I bought it FROM FRED*), Instrument (*Bill cut it WITH A KNIFE*), and Beneficiary (*I bought it FOR YOU*), as well as Time and Place.

No animal language in the wild has such structural features. At best, wild animal languages amount to a few dozen utterances and associated intensifiers (usually involving repetition, as in the circuits of the waggle dance or the repeats of a primate alarm cry), with combinations of utterances rarely utilized for new message types. With education, some animals have come to understand a consistent word order, so that they correctly respond to "Kanzi, touch the banana to the ball," in which word order is used to distinguish the actor from the acted upon.

Linguists, however, would like to place the language boundary well beyond such sentence comprehension: in looking at animal experiments, they want to see sentence *production* using a mental grammar; mere comprehension, they insist, is too easy. Though guessing at meaning often suffices for comprehension, the attempt to generate and speak a unique sentence quickly demonstrates whether or not you know the rules well enough to avoid ambiguities.

Yet that production test is more relevant to the scientist's distinctions than those of the language-learner's; after all, comprehension comes first in children. The original attempts to teach chimps the manual sign language of the deaf involved teaching the chimp how to produce the desired movements; comprehension of what the sign signified only came later, if at all. Now that the ape-language research has finally addressed the comprehension issue, it looks like more of a hurdle than anyone thought—but once an animal is past it, spontaneous production increases.

Linguists aren't much interested in anything simpler than real rules, but ethologists and the comparative and developmental psychologists are. Sometimes, to give everyone a piece of the action, we talk about languages plural, "language" in the sense of systematic communication, and Language with a capital L for the utterances of the advanced-syntax-using élite. All aid in the development of versatility and speed (and hence intelligence). While morphology and phonology also tell us something about cognitive processes, phrase structure, argument structure, and the relative-position words are of particular interest because of their architectural aspect—and that provides some insights about the mental structures available for the guessing-right type of intelligence.

> *Comprehension demands an active intellectual process of listening to another party while trying to figure out, from a short burst of sounds, the other's meaning and intent—both of which are always imperfectly conveyed. Production, by contrast, is simple. We know what we think and what we wish to mean. We don't have to figure out "what it is we mean," only how to say it. By contrast, when we listen to someone else, we not only have to determine what the other person is saying, but also what he or she means by what is said, without the insider's knowledge that the speaker has.*
>
> SUE SAVAGE-RUMBAUGH, 1994

How MUCH OF LANGUAGE is innate in humans? Certainly the drive to learn new words via imitation is probably innate in a way that a drive to learn arithmetic is not. Other animals learn gestures by imitation, but preschool children seem to average ten new words every day—a feat that puts them in a whole different class of imitators. And they're acquiring important social tools, not mere vocabulary: the right tool for the job, the British neuropsychologist Richard Gregory emphasizes, confers intelligence on its user—and words are social tools. So this drive alone may account for a major increment in intelligence over the apes.

There is also the drive of the preschooler to acquire the rules of combination we call mental grammar. This is not an intellectual task in the usual sense: even children of low-average intelligence seem to effortlessly acquire syntax by listening. Nor is acquisition of syntax a result of trial and error, because children seem to make fairly fast transitions into syntactic constructions. Learning clearly plays a role but some of the rigidities of grammar suggest innate wiring. As Derek Bickerton points out, our ways of expressing relationships (such as all those *above/below* words) are resistant to augmentation, whereas you can always add more nouns. Because of regularities across languages in the errors made by children just learning to speak, because of the way various aspects of grammar change together across languages (SVO uses prepositions such as "by bus," SOV tends to postpositions such as "bus by"), because of those adult Asian immigrants, and because of certain constructions that seem forbidden in any known language, linguists such as Noam Chomsky have surmised that something biological is involved—that the human brain comes wired for the treelike constructions needed for syntax, just as it is wired for walking upright:

> Normal speech consists, in large part, of fragments, false starts, blends and other distortions of the underlying idealized forms. Nevertheless . . . what the child learns is the underlying [idealized form]. This is a remarkable fact. We must also bear in mind that the child constructs this [idealized form] without explicit instruction, that he acquires this knowledge at a time when he is not capable of complex intellectual achievements in many other domains, and that this achievement is relatively independent of intelligence.

There is, of course, a "language module" in the brain—located just above the left ear in most of us—and Universal Grammar might be wired into it at birth. Monkeys lack this left lateral language area: their vocalizations (and the emotional utterances of humans) utilize a more primitive cortical speech area above the corpus callosum. Nobody knows yet whether apes have a lateral language area or similar arrangement.

IF A YOUNG BONOBO OR CHIMPANZEE had the two drives that young human children have—to seek out words and discover rules—in sufficient intensity and at the right time in brain development, would it self-organize a language cortex like ours and use it to crystallize a set of rules out of word mixtures? Or is that neural wiring innate in humans, there without the relevant experience and simply unused if the drives or opportunities are missing? Either, it seems to me, is consistent with the Chomskian claim. Universal Grammar might result from the "crystallization" rules of the self-organization, arising just as "flashers" and "gliders" do from cellular automata.

And the way you experimentally distinguish between uniquely human innate wiring and input-driven crystallization is to push vocabulary and sentences on promising ape students, with clever motivation schemes attempting to substitute for the child's untutored acquisitiveness. It is, I think, fortunate that the apes are borderline when it comes to having the linguists' True Language, because by studying their struggles we might eventually glimpse the functional foundations of mental grammar. In the course of human evolution, the stepping-stones may have been paved over, overlaid by superstructures and streamlined beyond recognition.

Sometimes ontogeny recapitulates phylogeny (the baby's attempts to stand up recapitulating the quadruped-to-biped phylogeny; the descent of the larynx in the baby's first year partially recapitulating the ape-to-human changes). Yet, development can happen so rapidly that you fail to see the reenactment of evolutionary progress. If we could see the transition to fancier constructions in bonobos, however, we might be able to discover what sorts of learning augment syntax, what other tasks compete and so hinder language, and what brain areas "light up" in comparison to those in humans. Besides the major implications for our view of what's uniquely human, an understanding of ape linguistic foundations might help us teach the language-impaired, and might even reveal synergies that would aid language learning and better guessing. It is only through the efforts of skilled teachers of bonobos that we're likely to answer questions about the stepping-stones.

SYNTAX IS WHAT YOU USE, it would appear, to make those fancier mental models, the ones involving who did what to whom, why, when, and with what means. Or at least if you want to communicate such an elaborate understanding, you'll have to translate your mental model of those relationships into the mental grammar of the language, then you order or inflect the words to help the listener reconstruct your mental model. It might, of course, be easier just to "think in syntax" in the first place. In that sense, we'd expect the augmentation of syntax to result in a great augmentation of guessing-right intelligence.

The name of the game is to re-create your mental model in the listener's mind. The recipient of your message will need to know the same mental grammar, in order to decode the string of words into approximately the same mental understanding. So syntax is about structuring relationships between items (words, usually) in your underlying mental model, not about the surface of things—such as SVO or inflections, which are mere clues. Your job as a listener is to figure out what sort of tree will provide an adequate fit to the string of words you hear. (Imagine being sent the numerical values for a spreadsheet and having to guess the spreadsheet formulas needed to interrelate them!)

The way this could work is that you try out a simple arrangement (actor, action, acted-upons, modifiers) and wind up with words left over. You try another tree, and discover that there are unfilled positions that can't be left empty. You use those clues about tree structure provided by the speaker's plurals and verbs—for example, you know that "give" requires both a recipient and an item given. If there is no word (spoken or implied) to fill a required slot, then you scratch that tree and go on to yet another. Presumably you try a lot of different trees simultaneously rather than seriatim, because comprehension (finding a good enough interpretation of that word string) can operate at blinding speed.

In the end, several trees may fill properly with no words left over, so you have to judge which of the interpretations is most reasonable given the situation you're in. Then you're finished. That's comprehension—at least in my (surely oversimplified) version of the linguists' model.

THINK IN TERMS OF A GAME OF SOLITAIRE: you're not finished until you have successfully uncovered all the face-down cards—while following the rules about descending order and alternate colors—and in some shuffles of the deck, it is impossible to succeed. You lose that round, shuffle the deck, and try again. For some word strings, no amount of rearranging will find a meaningful set of relationships—a story you can construct involving who did what to whom. If someone utters such an ambiguous word string to you, they've failed an important test of language ability.

For some sentences generated by a linguistically competent human, you have the opposite problem: you can construct multiple scenarios—alternative ways of understanding the word string. Generally, one of the candidates will satisfy the conventions of the language or the situation better than others, thus becoming the "meaning" of the communication. Context creates default meanings for some items in the sentence, saving the speaker from producing a longer utterance. (Pronouns are such a shortcut.)

The kind of formal rules of compositional correctness you learned in high school are, in fact, violated all the time in the incomplete utterances of everyday speech. But everyday speech suffices, because the real test is in whether you convey your mental model of who did what to whom to your audience, and the context will usually allow the listener to fill in the missing pieces. Because a written message has to function without much of the context, and without such feedback as an enlightened or puzzled look on the listener's face, we have to be more complete—indeed, more redundant—when writing than when speaking, making fuller use of syntax and grammatical rules.

LINGUISTS WOULD LIKE TO UNDERSTAND how sentences are generated and comprehended in a machinelike manner—what enables the blinding speed of sentence comprehension. I like to call this "language machine" a *lingua ex machina*. That does, of course, invite comparison with the *deus ex machina* of classical drama—a platform wheeled on stage (the god machine), from which a god lectured the other actors, and more recently the term bestowed on any contrived resolution of a plot difficulty. Until our "playwrighting" technique improves, our algorithms for understanding sentences will also seem contrived.

I'm going to propose how one such *lingua ex machina* could work, combining phrase structure and argument structure in an algorithmic way. Linguists will probably find it at least as contrived as other diagraming systems. But here's a few paragraphs' worth of Calvin's Vacuum-Lifter Package-Carrying System, involving processes as simple as those of a shipping department or production line.

Let us say we have just heard or read a complete sentence, "The tall blond man with one black shoe gave the other one to her." How do we make a mental model of the action? We need to box up some of the pieces, and prepositional phrases are a good place to start. Our machine knows all the prepositions and takes the nouns adjacent to them (the following noun if the sentence is English, the preceding noun if it's in Japanese) into the same box. I'll use boxes with rounded corners to indicate the packaging of phrases—"with one black shoe" and "to her." On occasion, nonlinguistic memories have to be brought to bear in order to box things up correctly, as in that ambiguous phrase "the cow with the crumpled horn that Farmer Giles likes." Knowing that Giles has a collection of horns over the fireplace could help you guess whether "that Farmer Giles likes" should be boxed with "cow" or with "crumpled horn."

Verbs get special boxes, because of the special role they play. Had there been an -*ly* word (an adverb), or an auxiliary, such as "must," I would have boxed them up with the verb, even if they weren't adjacent to it. Then we box up the noun phrases, incorporating any prepositional phrase boxes that modify them, so that we may have rounded boxes within rectangular boxes. If we have a nested phrase, it can function as a noun for purposes of the next boxing. Now we've got everything boxed up (there have to be at least two boxes but often there are more).

Next we've got to "lift" them as a group and metaphorically carry this amalgamation away from the work space, understood at last. Will it get off the ground? There are a few different types of handles in my vacuum-lifter machine, and

The Calvin Vacuum-Lifter Package-Carrying System

1. Box up your prepositional phrases, with a special box for the verb (including any adverbs, auxiliaries).

The tall blond man with one black shoe gave the other one to her.

2. Box up your noun phrases with any modifiers (boxes within boxes).

The tall blond man with one black shoe gave the other one to her.

3. The verb identifies a type of lifter handle: subject with two obligatory objects.

The tall blond man with one black shoe gave the other one to her.

4. Success is being able to "lift" the sentence, with nothing left over.

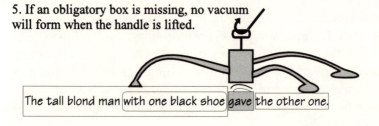

The tall blond man with one black shoe gave the other one to her.

5. If an obligatory box is missing, no vacuum will form when the handle is lifted.

The tall blond man with one black shoe gave the other one.

the one we must use depends on the verb we identified (in this case, the past tense of "give"). There is another vacuum sucker, for the noun phrase box containing the subject (I've drawn it as a little pyramid). You can't have a sentence without both a subject and a verb, and if the subject is missing, air will be sucked in the opening, no vacuum will form, and the package lifter won't lift. (That's why I've used suckers here rather than hooks—to make a target obligatory.)

But, as I noted earlier, "give" is peculiar, in that it requires two objects. (You can't say, "I gave to her." Or "I gave it."). Therefore this lift handle has two additional suction lines. I've also allowed it some nonvacuum lines—simple strings with hooks, which can carry as many optional noun phrases and prepositional phrases, however many that the verb allows.

Sometimes the suction tips and optional hooks need some guidance to find an appropriate target: for example, SVO might help the subject tip find the appropriate noun phrase—as might a case marker, such as "he." Other inflections help out, like gender or number agreement between verb and subject. The suction tips and the hooks could come with little labels on them for Beneficiary, Instrument, Negation, Obligation, Purpose, Possession, and so forth, mating only with words appropriate to those categories. Being able to lift the verb handle and carry all the packages, leaving none behind and with no unfilled suction tips, is what constitutes sentence recognition in this particular grammar machine. If a suction tip can't find a home, no vacuum develops when you lift the handle, and your construction isn't carried away. There's no sense of completion.

As noted, each verb, once identified by the *lingua ex machina*, has a characteristic handle type: for instance, handles for intransitive verbs such as "sleep" have only the one suction tip for the subject, but they have optional hooks, in case there are any extra phrases to be hauled along. "Sleep" will support optional roles such as Time ("after dinner") and Place ("on the sofa")—but not Recipient.

There's usually a vacuum tip for an Agent (though sometimes there isn't an Agent—say, in sentences like "The ice melted"), perhaps other role-related suction tips, and some

In addition to suction pipes for obligatory roles, many verb handles have "hooks" that carry optional roles, if they can find a box with appropriate content.

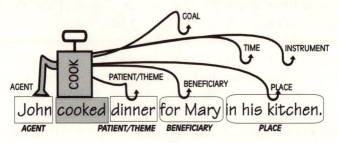

Intransitive verb handles lack certain role hooks....

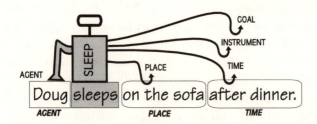

... and so some illegal boxes may have no lifters, causing a box to be left behind, the task incomplete.

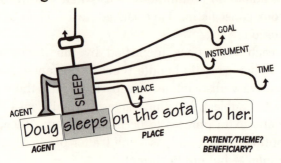

hooks for other possible roles in the verb's storytelling repertoire.

And, of course, the same boxes-inside-boxes principle that allowed a prepositional phrase to serve as a noun can allow us to have sentences inside sentences, as in dependent clauses or "I think I saw him leave to go home."

THAT'S THE SHORT VERSION of my package-carrying system. If it seems worthy of Rube Goldberg, remember that he's the patron saint of evolution.

I assume that, just as in a roomful of bingo players, many attempts at a solution are made in parallel, with multiple copies of the candidate sentence superimposed on different prototypical sentence scaffolds, and that most of these arrangements fail because of leftover words and unfilled suction tips. The version whose verb handle lifts everything shouts, "Bingo!" and the deciphering game is over (unless, of course, there's a tie).

Being able to lift everything is simply a test of a properly patterned sentence; note that, once lifted successfully, sequence and inflections no longer matter, because roles have been assigned. This *lingua ex machina* would lift certain kinds of nonsense—such as Chomsky's famous example, "Colorless green ideas sleep furiously"—but would, appropriately, fail to lift a nonsentence, such as "Colorless green ideas sleep them." (The "sleep" verb handle has no hooks or suckers for leftover Objects.)

Though a sensible mental model of relationships may be the goal of communication, and ungrammatical sentences cannot be deciphered except through simple word association, grammatical patterns of words can nonetheless be generated that fit sentence expectations but have no reasonable mental model associated with them. The test of semantics is different than the test of grammar. Semantics is also the tie-breaker, deciding among multiple winners, in somewhat the same way as boxing matches without a knockout are decided on judges' points. That's also how we guess what Farmer Giles is likely to like, the cow or the horn.

WHILE EACH SENTENCE IS A LITTLE STORY, we also build string-based conceptual structures far larger than sentences. They too have lots of obligatory and optional roles to fill. They come along in the wake of grammar, as the writer Kathryn Morton observes:

> The first sign that a baby is going to be a human being and not a noisy pet comes when he begins naming the world and demanding the stories that connect its parts. Once he knows the first of these he will instruct his teddy bear, enforce his world view on victims in the sandlot, tell himself stories of what he is doing as he plays and forecast stories of what he will do when he grows up. He will keep track of the actions of others and relate deviations to the person in charge. He will want a story at bedtime.

Our plan-ahead abilities gradually develop from childhood narratives and are a major foundation for ethical choices, as we imagine a course of action, imagine its effects on others, and decide not to do it.

By borrowing the mental structures for syntax to judge other combinations of possible actions, we can extend our plan-ahead abilities and our intelligence. To some extent, this is done by talking silently to ourselves, making narratives out of what might happen next, and then applying syntax-like rules of combination to rate (a decision on points, again) a candidate scenario as dangerous nonsense, mere nonsense, possible, likely, or logical. But our intelligent guessing is not limited to language-like constructs; indeed, we may shout, "Eureka!" when a set of mental relationships clicks into place, yet have trouble expressing this understanding verbally for weeks thereafter. What is it about human brains that allows us to be so good at guessing complicated relationships?

We do not realize how deeply our starting assumptions affect the way we go about looking for and interpreting the data we collect. We should recognize that nonhuman organisms need not meet every new definition of human language, tool use, mind, or consciousness in order to have versions of their own that are worthy of serious study. We have set ourselves too much apart, grasping for definitions that will distinguish man from all other life on the planet. We must rejoin the great stream of life from whence we arose and strive to see within it the seeds of all we are and all we may become.

SUE SAVAGE-RUMBAUGH, 1994

[We] can understand neither ourselves nor our world until we have fully understood what language is and what it has done for our species. For although language made our species and made the world we inhabit, the powers it unleashed drove us to understand and control our environment, rather than explore the mainspring of our own being. We have followed that path of control and domination until even the most daring among us have begun to fear where it may lead. Now the engine of our quest for power and knowledge should itself become the object that we seek to know.

DEREK BICKERTON, 1990

....

CHAPTER 6

EVOLUTION ON-THE-FLY

*Foresight of phenomena and power over them
depend on knowledge of their sequences, and not
upon any notion we may have formed respecting
their origin or inmost nature.*

JOHN STUART MILL,
Auguste Comte and Positivism, 1865

*The problems are solved, not by giving new
information, but by arranging what we have
known since long.*

LUDWIG WITTGENSTEIN,
Philosophical Investigations, 1953

"ONE THING FOLLOWS ANOTHER" is a fairly simple concept, one
that many animals can master. Indeed, it's what most learning
is all about; for Pavlov's dogs, it was *bell* tends to be followed
by *food*.

More than two things may be chained; many animals have
elaborate song sequences, not to mention all those elaborate
locomotion sequences, such as gaits. Acquiring vocabulary
and understanding basic word order are, we just saw, relatively easy language tasks for both humans and bonobos.

If sequence is so elementary, why is planning ahead so rare
in the animal kingdom, except for those trivial cases of fore-

sight that mere melatonin can handle so well? What additional mental machinery is required in order to plan for a novel contingency? (Perhaps argument structure, as in those verb-lifting handles?) How do we do something we've never done before, with no exact memories to guide us? How do we even imagine such a thing?

We are always saying something we've never said before. The other novelty generator, operating just as frequently in our lives (though often subconsciously), is that "What happens next?" predictor, mentioned in chapter 2 in the context of humor and the distressful effects of environmental incoherence.

Perhaps the mechanisms for foresight are similar to those used in the fancier aspects of mental grammar, the ones involving long-term dependencies, as when basic word order is replaced by the alternate forms for the who-what-when questions. Perhaps the trees used by phrase structure, or the obligatory roles of argument structure, are mental mechanisms that are useful for foresight in a more general way.

Mental grammar provides our most detailed set of insights into those mental structures that might be handy for intelligent guessing. This chapter will take a look at three more: chunking, sequencing, and darwinian processes.

JUGGLING A HALF-DOZEN THINGS at the same time is one of those abilities measured by multiple-choice tests, particularly analogy questions (A is to B as C is to [D, E, F]). It also shows up in our ability to remember phone numbers for a long enough time to dial them. Many people can hang on to a seven-digit number between five and ten seconds, but will resort to writing it down if faced with an out-of-area number or an even longer international one.

The limitation, it turns out, is not the number of digits; it's the number of *chunks*. I remember San Francisco's area code, 415, as a single chunk, but the number 451 means nothing to me, so I would have to remember it as three chunks: 4, 5, and 1. *Chunking* refers to the process of collapsing 4, 1, and 5 into the entity 415. A ten-digit San Francisco phone number, such as 4153326106, is, to me, only eight chunks; our schemes for using nondialed separators when writing down numbers—as in (415)332-6106 or 415.332.6106—are essentially aids to chunking. Since we are already familiar with many two-digit numbers as single words—for example, "nineteen"—the Parisian 42-60-31-25 style of separators makes for more easily memorized eight-digit number strings.

How many chunks can you hang onto? That varies among people, but the typical range forms the title of a famous 1956 paper by the psychologist George Miller: "The Magical Number Seven, Plus or Minus Two." It's as if the mind had room for only a limited number of items—at least, in the work space used for current problems. When you get close to your limit, you try to collapse several items into one chunk so as to make more room. Acronyms are a version of chunking, making one "word" from many. Indeed, many new words are just substitutes for a longer phrase, as when someone invented *ambivalence* as a shortcut, to save a whole paragraph of explanation. A dictionary is a compendium of chunking over the centuries. The combination of chunking and rapid speech, so that much meaning can be accommodated within the brief span of short-term memory, has surely been important for holding as much information as possible in mind at the same time.

So one of the first lessons about working memory is that there's seemingly a limited scratch pad, better suited to a half-dozen items than twice that number. This limitation probably has some implications for intelligence (certainly for IQ tests!), but the key feature of intelligent acts is creative divergent thinking, not memory per se. What we need is a process that will produce good guesses.

LANGUAGE AND INTELLIGENCE ARE SO POWERFUL that we usually assume that more and more would be better and better. Evolutionary theorists, however, are fond of demonstrating that evolution is full of dead-end stabilities that can prevent such straightforward "progress" and they like to point out evolution's indirect routes involving multipurpose organs. Many organs are actually multipurpose and change their relative mix of functions over time. (When did that gas exchange organ in fish, known as the "swim bladder" because of its role in neutralizing buoyancy, become a lung?) And, if the analogy to computer software is to be believed, it's far easier for the brain to be multipurpose than it is for any other organ system. Some *regions* of the brain are surely multipurpose too.

So, in asking about how neural machinery for foresight or language got started, we must bear in mind that the underlying mechanisms might serve multiple functions, any one of which could be driven by natural selection and so incidentally benefit the others. They might be like what architects call core facilities, such as the rooms for the photocopy machines and the mailboxes. The mouth, for example, is a multipurpose core facility involved with drinking, tasting, ingesting, vocalization, and emotional expression; in some animals, also with breathing, cooling off, and fighting.

Bundling (paying for one thing, but getting something else "free") is a familiar marketing strategy. What human abilities might come bundled together like the proverbial "free lunch" that comes with the cost of the drinks? In particular, might syntax or planning come bundled with some other ability, simply because they can make spare-time use of a core facility?

I realize that a "free lunch" explanation is going to offend the sensibilities of the more Calvinist of the strict adaptationists in evolutionary theory—the ones that think that every little feature has to pay its own way. But strict accounting isn't always the name of the game. As noted earlier (*enlarge one, enlarge them all*), mammalian brain enlargements tend not to come piecemeal. And a free lunch is just another way of looking at what the original adaptationist himself emphasized. Charles Darwin reminded his readers, in a caution to his general emphasis on adaptations, that conversions of function were "so important."

In the midst of converting function—swim bladder into lung, for example—there is likely a multifunctional period (indeed, the multifunctional period could last forever). During it, an anatomical feature formerly under natural selection for one function gives an enormous boost to some new function, far beyond whatever natural selection the new function has experienced so far. Lungs were "bootstrapped" by earlier buoyancy considerations. What brain functions have bootstrapped others, and does it tell us anything about intelligence?

> *In considering transitions of organs, it is so important to bear in mind the probability of conversion from one function to another.*
> CHARLES DARWIN, *The Origin of Species*, 1859

WE CERTAINLY HAVE A PASSION for stringing things together in structured ways, ones that go far beyond the sequences produced by other animals. Besides words into sentences, we combine notes into melodies, steps into dances, and elaborate narratives into games with procedural rules. Might structured strings be a core facility of the brain, useful for language, storytelling, planning ahead, games, and ethics? Might natural selection for *any* of these abilities augment the common neural machinery, so that improved grammar incidentally serves to expand plan-ahead abilities?

Some beyond-the-apes abilities—music, for example—are puzzling, because it is hard to imagine environments that would give the musically gifted an evolutionary advantage over the tone deaf. To some extent, music and dance are surely secondary uses of that very neural machinery that was shaped up by structured strings more exposed to natural selection, such as language.

What other beyond-the apes abilities were likely to have been under strong natural selection? As improbable as it initially seems, planning ballistic movements may have once promoted language, music, and intelligence. Apes have elementary forms of the rapid arm movements that we're experts at—hammering, clubbing, and throwing—and one can imagine hunting and toolmaking scenarios that in some settings were important additions to the basic hominid gathering and scavenging strategies. If the same "structured string" core facility is used for the mouth as is used for ballistic hand movements, then improvements in language might promote manual dexterity. It could work the other way, too: accurate throwing opens up the possibility of eating meat regularly, of being able to survive winter in the temperate zone—and of talking all the better as an incidental benefit, a "free lunch."

CHOOSING BETWEEN HAND MOVEMENTS involves finding a candidate movement program—likely a characteristic firing pattern of cortical neurons—and then some more candidates. Little is yet known about how this transpires in the human brain, but a simple model involves multiple copies of each movement program, each competing for space in the brain. The program for an open palm might make copies more readily than the program for making a V-sign or a precision pincer grip.

Ballistic movements (so named because beyond a certain point there is no opportunity to modify the command) require a surprising amount of planning, compared to most movements. They also likely require lots of clones of the movement program.

For sudden limb movements lasting less than about an eighth of a second, feedback corrections are largely ineffective, because reaction times are so long. Nerves conduct too slowly, and decisions aren't made quickly enough; feedback might help plan for next time, if the target hasn't run away by then, but it's no help in real time. For the last one-eighth second of clubbing, hammering, throwing, and kicking, the brain has to

Deciding on a Move

Three different candidates for a hand movement might compete for space in premotor cortex by cloning their spatio-temporal patterns.

Only when there was a sufficient chorus in one pattern might movement finally begin.

plan every detail of the movement and then spit it out, rather like punching a roll for a player piano and then letting it roll.

We need nearly complete advance planning for ballistic movements during "get set," with no reliance on feedback. Hammering requires planning the exact sequence of activation for dozens of muscles. In the case of throwing, the problem is difficult for an additional reason: there is a launch window—a range of times when the projectile can be released and still hit the target. Release occurs shortly after the velocity peaks, as the projectile sails out of the decelerating hand. Getting this peak velocity to occur at exactly the right time, at the appropriate angle from the horizontal, is the trick.

Given the launch-window problems, you can see why planning is so difficult for human ballistic movements. Launch windows depend on how far away the target is, and on how big it is. Let's say that, eight tries out of ten, you can hit a rabbit-sized target from the length of one parallel parking space—which implies a launch window of 11 milliseconds. Hitting the same target from twice the distance with equal reliability means releasing within a launch window about eight times narrower, 1.4 msec. Neurons are not exactly atomic clocks when it comes to timing accuracy; there is a lot of jitter when impulses are produced, enough so that any one neuron would have trouble hitting the broad side of a barn if it had to time the ball's release all by itself.

Happily, many noisy neurons are better than a few—so long as they're all "doing their own thing" and thereby making their own mistakes. Combining them can average out some of the noise. You can see this principle at work in the heart, making the heartbeat more regular. A fourfold increase in the number of pacemaker cells serves to cut the heartbeat jitter in half. To reduce ballistic release jitter eightfold requires averaging the output of 64 times as many noisy neurons as you needed to program the original throw. If you want to hit that same rabbit-sized target at three times the distance with that same eight-out-of-ten-times reliability, count on needing to recruit a lot of helpers: you will require 729 times as many neurons as the number sufficient for generating your standard short throw. It's redundancy, but in a different sense from, say, the three ways every large airplane has of lowering the landing gear.

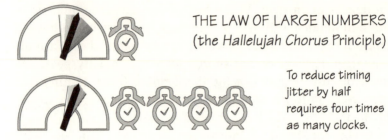

THE LAW OF LARGE NUMBERS
(the *Hallelujah Chorus* Principle)

To reduce timing jitter by half requires four times as many clocks.

So now we have a third insight into relevant brain mechanisms for fancy sequences: besides those trees and handles of syntax, besides those limited scratch-pad memories that encourage chunking, we see that fancy sequences of activation such as the ballistic movements probably share cerebral real estate with other fancy sequences—and that some need hundredfold levels of redundancy when precision timing is important.

Lots of planning space is also needed when you are throwing at a nonstandard target distance—one for which you don't have a stored movement plan (as you might for throwing darts or basketball free-throws). For nonstandard shots, you need to create an array of variants between two standard programs and pick the one that will come closest to hitting your target. Improvisation takes space. If, once you select the "best" variant, all the other variants change to conform to it, then you would have the redundancy needed for staying inside the launch window. Imagine a roomful of soloists, all singing somewhat different melodies and then converging on the one that they could sing as a chorus. And then, for real precision, recruiting a lot of helpers, just as the expert choir recruits the audience in the *Hallelujah Chorus*.

A core facility for structured sequences could solve a lot of problems. Does one actually exist? If so, we might occasionally see some synergy or conflict between similar movements.

CHARLES DARWIN WAS ONE OF THE FIRST to suggest hand-to-mouth synergies in his 1872 book on the expression of the emotions: "Thus persons cutting anything with a pair of scissors may be seen to move their jaws simultaneously with the blades of the scissors. Children learning to write often twist about their tongues as their fingers move, in a ridiculous fashion."

What kind of sequences are we talking about, anyway? Rhythmic movements per se are ubiquitous: chewing, breathing, locomotion, and so forth. They can be implemented by simple circuits at the level of the spinal cord. Like the simple one-thing-follows-another of learning, there is nothing distinctively cerebral about rhythm or other sequences. But *novel* sequences, that's the rub. If there is a common sequencer for the fancier novel movements, where is it located in the brain?

Sequencing in itself doesn't require a cerebral cortex. Much movement coordination in the brain is done at a subcortical level, in places known as the basal ganglia and the cerebellum. But novel movements tend to depend on the premotor and prefrontal cortex, in the rear two-thirds of the frontal lobes.

There are other regions of the cerebral cortex that are likely to be involved with sequential activities. The dorsolateral portions of the frontal lobe (dorso = top, lateral = side; if you had a pair of horns growing out of your forehead, these regions would lie beneath them) are crucial for delayed-response tasks. You show a monkey some food and allow him to watch where you hide it—but force him to wait twenty minutes before being allowed to go after it. Monkeys with damage to the dorsolateral frontal cortex will fail to retain that information. It may not be a failure of memory but a problem of formulating a lasting intention, perhaps even an "agenda."

The great Russian neurologist Alexander Luria described a patient in bed with his arms under the covers. Luria asked him to raise his arm. He couldn't seem to do that. But if Luria asked him to remove his arm from under the covers, he could do that. If Luria then asked him to raise his arm up and down in the air, the patient could do that, too. His difficulty was in planning the sequence—he got stuck on the condition of working around the obstacle of the confining bedcovers. Left prefrontal damage gives patients difficulty in unfolding a proper sequence of actions—or perhaps in planning them in the first place. Patients with damage to the left premotor cortex have trouble chaining the actions together into a fluent motion—what Luria called a kinetic melody.

Tumors or strokes in the bottom of the frontal lobe, just above the eyes, also affect sequences of activities, such as going shopping. One famous patient, an accountant, had a high IQ and did quite well on a battery of neuropsychological tests. Yet he had big problems in organizing his life: he was fired from a series of jobs, went bankrupt, and underwent two divorces in a two-year period as a result of impulsive marriages. Nonetheless, this man was often unable to make simple, rapid decisions—say, about what toothpaste to buy or what to wear. He would get stuck making endless comparisons and contrasts, often making no decision at all or a purely random one. If he wanted to go out for dinner, he had to consider the seating plan, the menu, the atmosphere, and the management of each possible restaurant. He might drive by them to see how busy they were, and even then would be unable to choose among them.

There are two major lines of evidence that suggest the lateral language area above the left ear also has a lot to do with nonlanguage sequencing. The Canadian neuropsychologist Doreen Kimura and her co-workers showed that left-lateral stroke patients with language difficulties (aphasia) also have considerable difficulty executing hand and arm movement sequences of a novel sort, a condition known as apraxia. (A fancy, though not novel, sequence would be taking your keys out of your pocket, finding the right one, inserting it into the lock, turning the key, and then pushing on the door.)

The Seattle neurosurgeon George Ojemann and his co-workers further showed, using electrical stimulation of the brain during epilepsy operations, that much of the left-lateral language specialization is involved with listening to sound sequences. These regions include the part of the frontal lobe adjacent to Broca's Area, the top of the temporal lobe on either side of the primary auditory cortex, and some of the parietal lobe in back of the map of the skin surface. (In other words, they're "perisylvian," bordering the Sylvian fissure.) The big surprise was that these exact same areas seem heavily involved in producing oral-facial movement sequences—even nonlan-

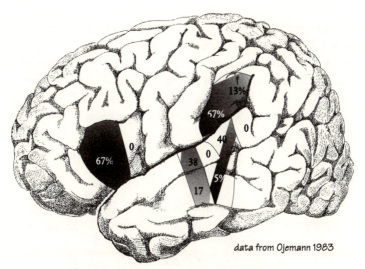

data from Ojemann 1983

Orofacial sequencing is disrupted
by electrical stimulation from the same
two zones as is phoneme perception.

guage ones, such as mimicking a series of facial expressions.

One of the hazards of naming things in the brain is that we expect something called the language cortex to be devoted to language. But data such as Ojemann's show that, at its core, the cortical specialization is far more generalized, concerned with novel sequences of various kinds: hand as well as mouth, sensation as well as movement, mimicry as well as narrative.

NOT ONLY CAN MANY SPECIES learn abstract symbols and a simple language, but some clearly can learn categories. Indeed, animals often overgeneralize, in the same way that a baby goes through a phase of calling all adult males "Daddy." Relationships can be learned, such as *is-a* or *is-larger-than*. A banana is a fruit, a banana is larger than a chestnut.

Closer to intelligence is the power of analogies, metaphors, similes, parables, and mental models. They involve the *comparing* of relationships, as when we make an imperfect analogy between *is-bigger-than* and *is-faster-than*, by inferring that *bigger-is-faster*.

We humans can mentally operate in a familiar domain (for example, filing a document in a file folder or throwing it in a wastebasket) and carry this relationship over to a less familiar domain (saving or deleting computer files, perhaps by means of moving icons on a screen). We can make a gesture in one mental domain and have it interpreted in another. These mappings all break down somewhere—and, in Robert Frost's words, we have to know how far we can ride a metaphor, judge when it's safe.

Consider the mapping from one domain to another that Umberto Eco creates here:

The fact is that the world is divided between users of the Macintosh computer and users of MS-DOS compatible computers. I am firmly of the opinion that the Macintosh is Catholic and that DOS is Protestant. Indeed, the Macintosh is counterreformist and has been influenced by the "ratio studiorum" of the Jesuits. It is cheerful, friendly, conciliatory, it tells the faithful how they must proceed step by step to reach—if not the Kingdom of Heaven—the moment in which their document is printed. It is catechistic: the essence of revelation is dealt with via simple formulae and sumptuous icons. Everyone has a right to salvation.

DOS is Protestant, or even Calvinistic. It allows free interpretation of scripture, demands difficult personal decisions, imposes a subtle hermeneutics upon the user, and takes for granted the idea that not all can reach salvation. To make the system work you need to interpret the program yourself: a long way from the baroque community of revelers, the user is closed within the loneliness of his own inner torment.

You may object that, with the passage to Windows, the DOS universe has come to resemble more closely the counterreformist tolerance of the Macintosh. It's true: Windows represents an Anglican-style schism, big ceremonies in the cathedral, but there is always the possibility of a return to DOS to change things in accordance with bizarre decisions. . . .

And machine code, which lies beneath both systems (or environments, if you prefer)? Ah, that is to do with the Old Testament, and is Talmudic and cabalistic.

Most mappings are simpler, as when objects are associated with a sequence of phonemes (as in naming). Chimpanzees, with some effort, can learn simple analogies, such as A is to B as C is to D. If the chimp could apply such mental manipulations to events in its everyday life, instead of using them only while at the testing apparatus, it would be a more capable ape. Humans, obviously, keep mapping into more and more abstract domains, notching stratified stability up a few more levels.

SAFETY IS THE BIG PROBLEM with trial combinations, ones that produce behaviors that have never been done before. Bigger isn't always faster. Even simple reversals in order can yield dangerous novelty, as in "Look *after* you leap." In 1943, in his book *The Nature of Explanation*, the British psychologist Kenneth Craik proposed that

> the nervous system is . . . a calculating machine capable of modeling or paralleling external events. . . . If the organism carries a "small-scale model" of external reality and of its own possible actions within its head, it is able to try out various alternatives, conclude which is the best of them, react to future situations before they arise, utilise the knowledge of past events in dealing with the future, and in every way to react in a much fuller, safer and more competent manner to the emergencies which face it.

Humans can simulate future courses of action and weed out the nonsense off-line; as the philosopher Karl Popper has said, this "permits our hypotheses to die in our stead." Creativity— indeed, the whole high end of intelligence and consciousness—involves playing mental games that shape up quality. What sort of mental machinery might it take to do something of the sort that Craik suggests?

THE AMERICAN PSYCHOLOGIST WILLIAM JAMES was talking about mental processes operating in a darwinian manner in the

1870s, little more than a decade after Charles Darwin published *On the Origin of Species*. The notion of trial and error was developed by the Scottish psychologist Alexander Bain in 1855, but James was using evolutionary thinking in addition.

Not only might darwinism shape up a better brain in two million years without the guiding hand of a master potter, but another darwinian process, operating in the brain, might shape up a more intelligent solution to a problem on the milliseconds-to-minutes timescale of thought and action. The body's immune response also appears to be a darwinian process, whereby antibodies that are better and better fits to the invading molecule are shaped up in a series of generations spanning several weeks.

Darwinian processes tend to start from the biological basic: reproduction. Copies are always happening. One theory of making up your mind is that you form some plans for movement—making an open hand, or a V-sign, or a precision pincer movement—and that these alternative movement plans reproductively compete with one another until one "wins." According to that theory, it takes a critical mass of command clones before any action is finally initiated.

Darwinism requires a lot more than just reproduction and competition, however. When I try to abstract the essential features of a darwinian process from what we know about species evolution and the immune response, it appears that a Darwin Machine must possess six essential properties, all of which must be present for the process to keep going:

- *It involves a pattern.* Classically, this is the string of DNA bases called a gene. As Richard Dawkins pointed out in *The Selfish Gene*, the pattern could also be a cultural one such as a melody, and he usefully coined the term *meme* for such patterns. The pattern could also be the brain activity patterns associated with thinking a thought.
- *Copies are somehow made* of this pattern. Cells divide. People hum or whistle a tune they've overheard. Indeed, the unit pattern (that's the meme) is defined by what's semi-reliably copied—for example, the gene's DNA sequence is

semi-reliably copied during meiosis, whereas whole chromosomes or organisms are not reliably copied at all.

- *Patterns occasionally change.* Point mutations from cosmic rays may be the best-known alterations, but far more common are copying errors and (as in meiosis) shuffling the deck.
- *Copying competitions occur* for occupation of a limited environmental space. For example, several variant patterns called bluegrass and crabgrass compete for my backyard.
- The *relative* success of the variants is influenced by a *multifaceted environment.* For grass, the operative factors are nutrients, water, sunshine, how often the grass is cut, and so on. We sometimes say that the environment "selects," or that there is selective reproduction or selective survival. Charles Darwin called this biasing by the term *natural selection.*
- The next generation is based on *which variants survive to reproductive age* and successfully find mates. The high mortality among juveniles makes their environment much more important than that of adults. This means that the surviving variants place their own reproductive bets from a shifted base, not from where the center of the variations was at conception (this is what Darwin called the inheritance principle). In this next generation, a spread around the currently successful is again created. Many new variants will be worse than the parental average, but some may be even better "fitted" to the environment's collection of features.

From all this, one gets that surprising darwinian drift toward patterns that almost seem designed for their environment. (There! I actually managed to work "intelligent design" into this intelligence book; maybe there's hope yet for "military intelligence.")

Sex (which is shuffling genes using two decks) isn't essential to the darwinian process, and neither is climate change—but they add spice and speed to it, whether it operates in milliseconds or millennia. A third factor accelerating the darwinian process is fragmentation and the isolation that follows: the darwinian process operates more quickly on islands than on continents. For some fancy darwinian processes requiring speed (and the timescale of thought and action certainly does), that might make fragmentation processes essential. A decelerating factor is a pocket of stability that requires considerable back-and-forth rocking in order to escape from it; most stable species are trapped in such stabilizing pockets.

People are always confusing particular parts, such as "natural selection," with the darwinian whole. But no one part by itself will suffice. Without all six essentials, the process will shortly grind to a halt.

People also associate the darwinian essentials exclusively with biology. But selective survival, for example, can be seen when flowing water carries away the sand and leaves the pebbles behind. Mistaking a part for the process ("Darwinism is selective survival") is why it has taken a century for scientists to realize that thought patterns may also need to be repeatedly copied—and that copies of thoughts may need to compete with copies of alternative ones on "islands" during a series of mental "climate changes" in order to rapidly evolve an intelligent guess.

IN OUR SEARCH for suitable brain mechanisms for guessing intelligently, we now have (1) those nested boxes of syntax that underlie strings; (2) argument structure with all its clues about probable roles; (3) those relative position words such as *near-into-above*; (4) the limited size of scratch-pad memory and the consequent chunking tendencies; and (5) common core facilities for fancy sequences, with quite a lot of need for extra copies of the neural patterns used to produce ballistic movements. Our sixth clue, from darwinian processes, now appears to be a whole suite of features: distinctive patterns, copying them, establishing variants via errors (with most of the variants coming from the most successful), competition, and the biasing of copying competitions by a multifaceted environment. What's more, it looks as if the multifaceted environment is partly remembered and partly current.

Fortunately, there is some overlap of darwinian considerations with those from the ballistic movements: darwinian backyard work spaces might utilize the "get set" scratch pads, and darwinian copying could help produce the jitter-reducing movement command clones. What else might correspond? In particular, what are those patterns that we might need to clone, on the timescale of thought and action?

THOUGHTS ARE COMBINATIONS of sensations and memories—or, looked at another way, thoughts are movements that haven't happened yet (and maybe never will). They're fleeting and mostly ephemeral. What does this tell us?

The brain produces movements by means of a barrage of nerve impulses going to the muscles, whether of the limbs or the larynx. Each muscle is activated at a somewhat different time, often only briefly; the whole sequence is timed as carefully as the finale of a fireworks display. A plan for a movement is like a sheet of music or a player-piano roll. In the latter case, the plan covers eighty-eight output channels and the times at which each key is struck, and, indeed, the ballistic movements involve almost as many muscles as the piano has notes. So a movement is a spatiotemporal pattern not unlike a musical refrain. It might repeat over and over, like the rhythms of locomotion, but it could also be more like a one-shot arpeggio, triggered by another temporal pattern.

Some spatiotemporal patterns in the brain probably qualify for the name *cerebral code*. Though individual neurons are more sensitive to some features of an input than others, no single neuron represents your grandmother's face. Just as your sense of a color depends on the *relative* activity in three different cone pathways from the retina, and a taste can be represented by the *relative* amounts of activity in about four different types of tongue receptors, so any one item of memory is likely to involve a committee of neurons. A single neuron, like any one key on the piano, is likely to play different roles in different melodies (most often, of course, its role is to keep quiet—again, like a piano key).

A cerebral code is probably the spatiotemporal activity pattern in the brain which represents an object, an action, or an abstraction such as an idea—just as bar codes on product packages serve to represent without resembling. When we see a banana, various neurons are stirred by the sight: some of the neurons happen to specialize in the color yellow, others in the short straight lines tangent to the banana's curve. Evoking a memory is simply reconstituting such a pattern of activity, according to the cell-assembly hypothesis put forward in 1949 by the Canadian psychologist Donald O. Hebb.

Mapping the Cell Assembly onto a Musical Scale

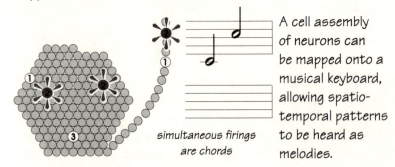

A cell assembly of neurons can be mapped onto a musical keyboard, allowing spatio-temporal patterns to be heard as melodies.

simultaneous firings are chords

So, the banana committee is like a melody, if we imagine the neurons involved as unpacked along a musical scale. Some neurophysiologists think that the involved neurons all have to fire synchronously, as in a chord, but I think that a cerebral code is more like a short musical melody, comprised of chords and individual notes; we neurophysiologists just find it easier to interpret chords than we do scattered single notes. What we really need are the families of strange attractors associated with words, but that's another book! (*The Cerebral Code.*)

> *Music is the effort we make to explain to ourselves how our brains work. We listen to Bach transfixed because this is listening to a human mind.*
> Lewis Thomas, *The Medusa and the Snail*, 1979

WE KNOW THAT LONG-TERM MEMORIES cannot be spatio*temporal* patterns. For one thing, they survive even massive shutdowns of the electrical activity in the brain, as in seizures or coma. But we now have lots of examples of how to convert a spatial pattern into a spatiotemporal one: musical notation, player pianos, phonograph records—even bumps in a washboarded road waiting for a car to come along and re-create a bouncing spatiotemporal pattern.

This is what Donald Hebb called dual-trace memory: a short-term active version (spatiotemporal) and a long-term spatial-only version similar to a sheet of music or the grooves on a phonograph record.

Some of these "cerebral ruts" are as permanent as those in the grooves of a phonograph record. The bumps and ruts are, essentially, the strengths of the various synapses that predispose the cerebral cortex to produce a repertoire of spatiotemporal patterns, much like the connection strengths in the spinal cord predispose it to produce the spatiotemporal patterns we know as walking, trotting, galloping, running, and so forth. But short-term memories can be either active spatiotemporal patterns (probably what is called "working memory" in the psychology literature) or transient spatial-only patterns— temporary ruts that somewhat overwrite the permanent ruts but don't vibrate (they merely fade in a matter of minutes). They're simply the altered synaptic strengths (what is called "facilitation" and "long-term potentiation" in the neurophysiological literature), the bumps left behind by a repetition or two of the characteristic spatiotemporal pattern.

The truly persistent bumps and ruts are unique to the individual, even to each identical twin, as the American psychologist Israel Rosenfield explains:

> Historians constantly rewrite history, reinterpreting (reorganizing) the records of the past. So, too, when the brain's coherent responses become part of a memory, they are organized anew as part of the structure of consciousness. What makes them memories is that they become part of that structure and thus form part of the sense of self; my sense of self derives from a certainty that my experiences refer back to *me,* the individual who is having them. Hence the sense of the past, of history, of memory, is in part the creation of the self.

COPYING IS GOING TO BE NEEDED over long distances in the brain. Like a fax machine, the brain must take a pattern and make a distant copy of it, perhaps on the other side of the brain. The pattern cannot be physically transported in the manner of a letter, so telecopying is likely to be important when the visual cortex wants to tell the language area that an apple has been seen. The need for copying suggests that the pattern we seek is the working memory, that active spatio*temporal* pattern, since it is difficult to see how "ruts" would otherwise copy themselves at a distance.

A darwinian model of mind and my analysis of the activity of throwing suggest that many clones might be needed locally, not just a few in distant places. Furthermore, in a darwinian process, an activated memory must somehow compete with other spatiotemporal patterns for occupation of a work space. And the other question we must answer is, What decides if one such "melody" is better than another?

Suppose a spatiotemporal pattern, produced in one little part with the aid of some appropriate "ruts," manages to induce the same melody in another cortical area that lacks those ruts. But the pattern can nonetheless be performed there, thanks to the active copying process nearby, even if it might not sustain itself without the driving patterns, the same way a square dance might fizzle out without a caller. If an adjacent area has bumps and ruts that are "close enough," the melody might catch on better, and die out less readily, than some other imposed melody. So resonating with a passive memory could be the aspect of the multifaceted environment that biases a competition.

In this way, the permanent bumps and ruts bias the competition. But so do the fading ones that were made by spatiotemporal activity patterns in that same patch of cortex a few minutes earlier. So, too, do the current active inputs to the region from elsewhere—the ones that are (like most synaptic inputs) in themselves too weak to induce a melody or create ruts. Probably most important is the background of secretions from the four major diffuse projection systems, the ones associated with the serotonin, norepinephrine, dopamine, and acetylcholine neuromodulators. Other emotional biases surely come from the neocortical projections of the such subcortical brain sites as the amygdala. Thalamic and cingulate gyrus inputs may bias competitions elsewhere, in the name of shifting your attention from external to memorized environments. Thus the current real-time environment, memories of near-past and long-past environments, emotional state, and attention all change the resonance possibilities, all likely bias the competition that shapes up a thought. Yet they could do it without themselves forming up clones to compete for cortical territory.

THE PICTURE THAT EMERGES from such theoretical considerations is one of a quilt, some patches of which enlarge at the expense of their neighbors as one code copies more successfully than another. As you try to decide whether to pick an apple or a banana from the fruit bowl (so my theory goes), the cerebral code for apple may be having a cloning competition with the one for banana. When one code has enough active copies to trip the action circuits, you might reach for the apple.

But the banana codes need not vanish; they could linger in the background as subconscious thoughts, undergoing variations. When you unsuccessfully try to remember someone's name, the candidate codes might continue copying for the next half hour, until suddenly Jane Smith's name seems to "pop into your mind," because your variations on the spatio-temporal theme finally hit a resonance good enough to generate a critical mass of identical copies. Our conscious thought may be only the currently dominant pattern in the copying competition, with many other variants competing for dominance, one of which will win a moment later, when your thoughts seem to shift focus.

It may be that darwinian processes are only the frosting on the cognitive cake; it may be that much is routine or rule-bound. But we often deal with novel situations in creative ways, as when you decide what to fix for dinner tonight. You survey what's already in the refrigerator and on the kitchen shelves. You think about a few alternatives, keeping track of what else you might have to fetch from the grocery store. All this can flash through your mind within seconds—and that's probably a darwinian process at work, as is speculating about what tomorrow might bring.

*We build mental models that represent
significant aspects of our physical and social
world, and we manipulate elements of those
models when we think, plan, and try to explain
events of that world. The ability to construct and
manipulate valid models of reality provides
humans with our distinctive adaptive advantage;
it must be considered one of the crowning
achievements of the human intellect.*
      GORDON H. BOWER and DANIEL G. MORROW, 1990

*Conflicts of representation are painful for a
variety of reasons. On a very practical level, it is
painful to have a model of reality that conflicts
with those of the people around you. The people
around you soon make you aware of that. But
why should this conflict worry people, if a model
is only a model, a best guess at reality that each
of us makes? Because nobody thinks of it in that
way. If the model is the only reality you can
know, then that model is reality, and if there is
only one reality, then the possessor of a different
model must be wrong.*
      DEREK BICKERTON, 1990

CHAPTER 7

···

SHAPING UP AN INTELLIGENT ACT
FROM HUMBLE ORIGINS

*The schematicism by which our understanding
deals with the phenomenal world . . . is a skill so
deeply hidden in the human soul that we shall
hardly guess the secret trick that Nature here
employs.*
 Immanuel Kant, *Kritik der reinen Vernunft*, 1787

*"Why," said the Dodo, "the best way to explain it
is to do it."*
 Lewis Carroll, *Alice's Adventures in
 Wonderland*, 1865

Is this chapter really necessary? Well, no—in the sense that
many people could skip to the last chapter without realizing
that something was missing.

It all depends on how satisfied you are with organization
charts. Some people don't want to know any more. "Skip the
details," they say, "and just stick with the executive summary." But this chapter really isn't about the details omitted
from the last chapter—it's written from a different perspective, bottom-up rather than inferred from principles.

Principles are, unfortunately, rather like organization

charts—a sketchy, convenient fiction. Real organizations have a flow of information and decision making that isn't captured by the boxes and labels. Charts fail to take account of *people* and how they talk to one another, fail to take account of the "institutional memory." They fail to take account of how experts can also be generalists, of how decisions taken at one level interact with those taken at another. Any schematic account of the brain will share the shortcomings of organization charts.

This account of intelligence has, so far, failed to take much account of *neurons*—the nerve cells of the brain—and how *they* talk to one another, how they remember past events, how they collectively make decisions on a local and regional scale. Some of that simply isn't known yet, but it is certainly possible to sketch out a plausible account of copying competitions among the cerebral codes.

Whenever you are talking science, a good general rule is always to give a specific example—even if it is only a possible mechanism rather than a well-established one.

That's what this chapter provides: an example of how our cerebral cortex might function as a Darwin Machine and, in the process, create that constantly shifting focus of consciousness, even those subconscious thoughts that every so often pop into the foreground, unbeckoned. It shows how we might achieve the off-line ability to simulate our future actions in the real world—an ability that is the essence of guessing-right intelligence.

The inability to imagine a mechanism that could produce mind is at the heart of many of the Janitor's Dream and the mind-in-a-computer objections. This chapter describes the building blocks with which I can imagine how a thinking machine could be constructed. Your mileage may vary—but here's your chance, just one chapter long, to see a bottom-up mechanistic example of how our mental lives might operate, both consciously and subconsciously, both for the novel and the routine.

GRAY MATTER ISN'T REALLY GRAY, except in a dead brain; in a living brain, it has a rich blood supply. Think of those rivers that

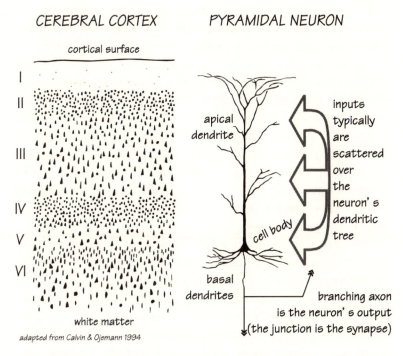

CEREBRAL CORTEX

cortical surface

PYRAMIDAL NEURON

I
II
III
IV
V
VI

white matter

adapted from Calvin & Ojemann 1994

apical dendrite

cell body

basal dendrites

inputs typically are scattered over the neuron's dendritic tree

branching axon is the neuron's output (the junction is the synapse)

run reddish-grayish-brown after a thunderstorm, and you'll have the right hue for the dynamic "gray matter."

The white matter in the brain, however, is really white, a porcelain hue, because of the fat that insulates the long, stringy part of a neuron. This part, which is called the "axon," is analogous to a wire and carries the neuron's output signal to near and distant targets. "Myelin" is the proper name for its fatty insulation. White matter is simply wire bundles, going every which way, much as you would see in the basement of a telephone-central-office building. The bulk of the brain is insulated wires connecting the parts that do the hard work, which are far smaller.

At one end of the axon is the neuron's cell body, the globular part of the cell containing the nucleus, with the DNA blueprints for the cell's day-to-day operation and maintenance. There are lots of treelike branches, called dendrites, arising from the cell body. Because cell bodies and dendrites lack the white insulation, large collections of them look "gray." The far end of a neuron's axon appears to be touching the dendrite of a downstream neuron—though, if you look carefully with an electron microscope, you'll see a little gap between the two cells called a synapse. Into this no-man's-land the upstream neuron releases a little neurotransmitter, which drifts across the gap and opens up some channels through the membrane of the downstream neuron. (Though there are some retrograde neurotransmitters in addition, a synapse is usually a one-way street, so it's useful to refer to "upstream" and "downstream" neurons.)

Overall, a single neuron looks like a bush, or the root of some herb such as ginger. It is the typical unit of computation, summing up the influences of a few thousand inputs—most of them excitatory, and some of them inhibitory, like deposits and checks—and speaking, in a single voice, to several thousand hardwired listeners.

The message sent from this "checking account" mostly concerns its "account balance" and how fast that balance is increasing. No message is sent unless the balance exceeds some threshold. Big deposits generate big messages, like interest payments with a bonus. But, just as piano keys don't produce any sound unless struck hard enough, cortical neurons are usually silent unless input conditions are surging—and then their output is proportional to how much they're stimulated by that account balance. (Oversimplified binary models usually treat a neuron as more like a harpsichord key, with a threshold but no gradation in volume for harder hits.)

Though the messages from short neurons can be simpler, neurons with axons longer than about 0.5 mm always utilize a signal booster: the *impulse*, a brief up-and-down voltage change of a standard size (like the loudness of that harpsichord key). Amplified and fed into a loudspeaker, the impulse sounds like a click (and we talk of the neuron "firing"). To get around the standard-size limitation, impulses usually repeat at a rate proportional to the account balance, the same way that a few quick repetitions of a harpsichord note may imitate a hard-struck piano note. Sometimes—especially in the cerebral cortex—just a few inputs, out of thousands, can conspire to trigger an impulse.

THE REALLY INTERESTING GRAY MATTER is that of the cerebral cortex, because that's where most of the novel associations are thought to be made—where the sight of a comb, say, is matched up to the feel of a comb in your hand. The cerebral codes for sight and feel are different, but they become associated somehow in the cortex, along with those for hearing the sound /kōm/ or hearing the characteristic sounds that the teeth of a comb make when they're plucked. You can, after all, identify a comb in any of these ways. It's hypothesized that there are specialized places in the cortex, called "convergence zones for associative memories," where those different modalities come together.

On the production side, you have linked cerebral codes for pronouncing /kōm/ and for generating the movements that manipulate a comb through the hair on your head. So between the sensory version of the word "comb" and the various movement manifestations, we expect to find a dozen different cortical codes associated with combs.

The cortical areas that do all this associating for us are a thin layer of icing on the cake of the white matter. The cerebral cortex is only about 2 mm thick, though it is deeply wrinkled. The *neocortex* (which is all of the cerebral cortex except for the hippocampus and some of the olfactory areas) has a surprisingly uniform packing density (with the exception of one layer of the primary visual cortex). If you made a grid atop the cortical surface, each square millimeter would have about 148,000 neurons beneath it—whether it was language cortex or motor cortex. But a sideways look, at the layers within that 2 mm depth, reveals some regional differences.

It's the icing of this cake that contains the layers, not the cake itself. A better bakery analogy might be a flaky pie crust made of croissantlike layers. The deepest layers are like an *out*-box, their wires mostly heading out of the cortex, bound for distant subcortical structures, such as the thalamus or the spinal cord. The middle layer is an *in*-box, with wires arriving from the thalamus and other such places. The superficial layers are like an *interoffice*-box; they make "corticocortical" connections with the superficial layers of other regions, both adjacent and distant. It's their axons that go through the corpus callosum to the other side of the brain—but most of the interoffice mail is delivered locally, within several millimeters. Such axon branches run sideways, rather than detouring through the white matter like the longer "U-fiber" branches.

Some regions have big in-boxes and small out-boxes, just like the ones to be found on the editorial-department desk that deals with letters to the editor. Superimposed on this stacked horizontal organization, moreover, is a fascinating set of vertical arrangements, similar to newspaper columns.

IF WE GO AROUND WIRETAPPING the individual neurons in the cerebral cortex, we discover that neurons with similar interests tend to be vertically arrayed there, forming cylinders known as cortical columns, which cut through most of the layers. It's almost like a club that self-organizes out of a crowd at a party, where people of similar interests tend to cluster together. We have naturally given names to these cortical clubs. Some of the names reflect their size, some their seeming specialties (so far as we know them).

The thin cylinders, or *minicolumns,* are only about 0.03 mm in diameter (that's a very thin hair, closer to the threads of

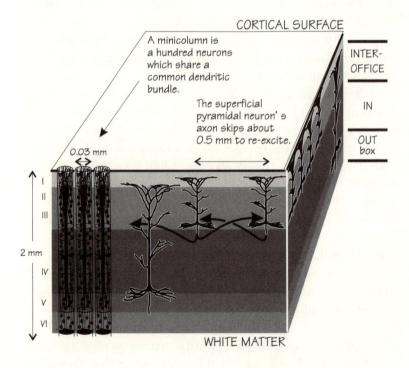

a spider web). The best-known examples of these are the visual cortex's orientation columns, whose neurons seem to like visual objects with a line or border tilted at a particular angle. The neurons in one minicolumn will respond best to boundaries tilted at 35°, those in another will like horizontals or verticals, and so forth.

You can look in a microscope and see (well, it takes some doing, even after a century of progress in neuroanatomical technique) a group of cortical neurons bundled together like stalks of celery. There is a tall "apical dendrite" that stretches up toward the cortical surface from the cell body (which is often triangular in appearance, hence the name "pyramidal neuron"). It is those apical dendrites of the pyramidal neurons that are bundled together, with 0.03 mm between adjacent bundles. There are about a hundred neurons in a minicolumn organized around one of those bundles, though the bundle at any one level might only have a dozen apical dendrites in it. Bundling is commonplace outside visual cortex, so minicolumns are likely a common element of cortical organization, just from the anatomy—but elsewhere we are ignorant of what the neurons of a minicolumn are "interested in."

Other "interest groups" tend to be much larger and comprised of more than a hundred minicolumns; these so-called *macrocolumns* are 0.4–1.0 mm across (that's a thin pencil lead) and sometimes appear more like elongated curtain folds than like proper cylinders. Such macrocolumns seem to result from an organization of the inputs—for example, in visual cortex those axons carrying information from the left eye tend to alternate every 0.4 mm with those being relayed from the right eye. Inputs from other parts of the cortex itself tend to do the same thing; for example, looking at the cortical area just in front of the corpus callosum, you can see the inputs from the prefrontal cortex forming a macrocolumn, flanked on either side by macrocolumns formed by a clustering of parietal-lobe inputs.

The cortical neurons interested in color tend to cluster together (though not exclusively) in "blobs." Unlike macrocolumns, blobs don't extend through all layers of the cortex; they're found only in the superficial layers—up there with the interoffice mail. And they're not exclusively comprised of color specialists: perhaps only 30 percent of the neurons in a blob are color sensitive. The distances between blobs are similar (if not identical) to the those of the macrocolumns.

NEXT LEVEL OF ORGANIZATION? On the basis of layer thickness changing, there are fifty-two "Brodmann Areas" in each human hemisphere. At a boundary between Areas, you'll see the relative thickness of those interoffice-in-out stacked boxes change, as if the relative amounts of incoming, outgoing, and interoffice mail differed on adjacent "desks."

Area 17 is better known as the primary visual cortex, but generally it is premature to put functional labels on these areas in the manner of departments on an organization chart (Area 19, for example, has a half-dozen functional subdivisions). A Brodmann Area averages 21 cm² in unwrinkled area. If the visual cortex ratio holds elsewhere, that's on the order of 10,000 macrocolumns and a million minicolumns in the average cortical area.

That factor of a hundred keeps recurring: a hundred neurons to a minicolumn, roughly a hundred minicolumns to a macrocolumn, a hundred times a hundred macrocolumns to a cortical area (which makes me wonder if we're missing an intermediate "super-column" or "mini-area" organization on the scale of a hundred macrocolumns), and there are just over a hundred Brodmann Areas when you total those in both cerebral hemispheres.

Can we extend this hundredfold multiplier further? It does put us into the scale of social organizations: What's a hundred brains? That suggests certain legislative bodies such as the U.S. Senate. And the United Nations is representative of more than a hundred legislatures.

PERMANENT ELEMENTS OF BRAIN ORGANIZATION, such as cortical areas or minicolumns, are nice to know about. But we also need to understand those temporary work spaces of the brain—something closer to scratch pads and buffers—that are likely superimposed on the more permanent forms of anatomical organization.

To deal with the novel, we are indeed going to need some

empirical types of organization, like those hexagonal cells that form in the cooking oatmeal when you forget to stir it—forms that are used temporarily and then disappear. Occasionally these forms of organization are recalled to life if some aspect of them earlier formed enough "ruts" in the landscape of interconnection strengths—in which case the empirical organization became a new memory or habit.

In particular, we need to know about the *cerebral codes*—those patterns that represent each of the words of our vocabulary, and so forth—and what creates them. At first, it appears that we are dealing with a four-dimensional pattern—the active neurons scattered through three-dimensional cortex, as they perform in time. But largely because the minicolumns seem to organize all the cortical layers around similar interests, most people working on cortex think of it as a two-dimensional sheet, rather like the retina (yes, the retina is 0.3 mm thick and is subdivided into a few layers, but the mapping is clearly for a two-dimensional image).

So we can try thinking of two dimensions, plus time, for cortex (which is, of course, the way we apprehend the images on a movie screen or computer terminal)—perhaps with transparent overlays when the different cortical layers do different things. Just imagine the human cortex flattened out on those four sheets of typing paper like pie crust, with little patches lighting up like message-board pixels. What patterns will we observe when that cortex is seeing a comb? When the word "comb" is heard, or said? When the cortex is commanding a hand to comb the hair?

Memory recall may consist of the creation of a spatiotemporal sequence of neuron firings—probably a sequence similar to the firing sequence at the time of the input to memory, but shorn of some of the nonessential frills that promoted it. The recalled spatiotemporal pattern would be something like a message board in a stadium, with lots of little lights flashing on and off, creating an overall pattern. A somewhat more general version of such a Hebbian cell assembly would avoid anchoring the spatiotemporal pattern to particular cells, to make it more like the way the message board can scroll. The pattern continues to mean the same thing, even when it's implemented by different lights.

Though we tend to focus on the lights that turn on, note that lights that stay off also contribute to the pattern; if they are turned on randomly—by seizures, for example—they fog the pattern. Something similar to this fogging seems to happen in concussions: while an injured football player is being helped off the field, he can often tell you what play he was running, but ten minutes later he can't remember what happened to him. Injury slowly causes a lot of neurons to "light up," and patterns therefore become obscured in the manner of bright fog—what mountain climbers call "whiteouts." (Just remember: blackouts are sometimes from whiteouts.)

WHAT'S THE MOST ELEMENTARY PATTERN THAT MEANS SOMETHING? A major clue, it seems to me, is that pattern *copying* is needed, for various reasons.

Before DNA leapt to prominence, geneticists and molecular biologists were searching for a molecular structure that was capable of being reliably copied during cell division. One of the reasons that the double helix structure was so deeply satisfying when it was discovered in 1953 by Crick and Watson (and I write this while temporarily at the University of Cambridge, just across the courtyard from the building where they worked) was that it provided a way of making a copy, via the complementary pairs of DNA bases (C bonds with G, A pairs with T). Unzip the double helix into two separate halves and each DNA position on a half-zipper will soon be paired with another of its opposite type, just from all the loose ones floating around in the nucleotide soup. This gives you two identical double helices, where there was only one before. This copying principle paved the way for the understanding of the genetic code (how those DNA triplets "represented" the amino acid string that folds up into a protein) a few years later.

Is there a similar copying mechanism for cerebral activity patterns, and might it help us identify the most relevant of the Hebbian cell assemblies? That's the one we could properly call the cerebral code because it is the most elementary way of representing something (a particular connotation of a word, an imagined object, and so forth).

Copying hasn't been observed in the brain yet—we don't currently have tools of sufficient spatial and temporal resolution, though we're close. But there are three reasons why I think it's a safe bet.

- The strongest argument for the existence of copying is the darwinian process itself, which is inherently a copying competition biased by a multifaceted environment. It's so elementary a method for shaping up randomness into something fancy that it would be surprising if the brain didn't use it.
- Copying is also what's needed for precision ballistic movements, such as throwing—those dozens-to-hundreds of clones of the movement-command patterns that are required to hit the launch window.
- Then there's that *faux* fax argument of the last chapter: communication within the brain requires the telecopying of patterns.

Since 1991, my favorite candidate for a local neural circuit that could make copies of spatiotemporal patterns has been the mutually reinforcing circuitry of the interoffice-mail layers. The wiring of those superficial layers of cerebral cortex is, in a word, peculiar. Indeed, to a neurophysiologist, almost alarming. I look at those circuits and wonder how runaway activity is reined in, why seizures and hallucinations aren't frequent events. But those same circuits have some crystallization tendencies that ought to be particularly good at cloning spatiotemporal patterns.

OF THE HUNDRED NEURONS IN A MINICOLUMN, about thirty-nine are superficial pyramidal neurons (that is, their cell bodies reside in the superficial layers II and III). It's their circuitry that is peculiar.

Like all other pyramidal neurons, they secrete an excitatory neurotransmitter, usually glutamate. There's nothing peculiar about glutamate per se; it's one of the amino acids, more typically used as a building block of peptides and proteins. Diffusing across the synapse, the glutamate opens up several types of ion channels through the membrane of the next cell's dendrite. The first channel specializes in letting sodium ions through; that in turn raises the internal voltage of the downstream neuron.

A second downstream channel activated by glutamate is known as the NMDA channel, and it allows calcium ions into the downstream neuron along with some more sodium. NMDA channels are particularly interesting to neurophysiologists because they contribute to so-called long-term potentiation (LTP), a change in synaptic strength that endures for some minutes in neocortex. (Minutes, actually, are closer to the neurophysiological "short-term," but LTP sometimes lasts days in the hippocampus—which is an older and simpler version of cortex—and that's where the "long-term" name originated.)

LTP occurs when there is near synchrony (within dozens to hundreds of milliseconds) of several inputs to the downstream neuron; it simply turns up the "loudness control" for those inputs for a few minutes. These are the "bumps and ruts" that temporarily make it easier to re-create a particular spatiotemporal pattern. LTP is our best candidate for a short-term memory that can survive a distraction. It is also thought to contribute the scaffolding for the construction of truly long-lasting structural changes in synapses—the permanent bumps and ruts that aid in the re-creation of long-unused spatiotemporal patterns.

The interoffice layers are where most of the NMDA channels are located, and where most of the neocortical LTP occurs. These superficial layers have two more peculiarities, both of them having to do with the connections that their pyramidal neurons make with one another. On average, a cortical neuron contacts fewer than 10 percent of all neurons within a radius of 0.3 mm. But roughly 70 percent of the excitatory synapses on any superficial-layer pyramidal neuron are derived from pyramidal neurons less than 0.3 mm away, so these neurons may be said to have an unusually strong propensity to excite one another. To a neurophysiologist, that raises all sorts of red flags: it's a perfect setup for instability and wild oscillations, unless it's carefully regulated.

There is also a peculiar patterning to these "recurrent exci-

tatory" connections—a patterning not seen in the lower cortical layers. The axon of a superficial pyramidal neuron travels
sideways a characteristic distance without making any
synapses with other neurons, and then it produces a tight terminal cluster. Like an express train, it skips intermediate
stops. In the primary visual cortex, the distance from the cell
body to the center of the terminal cluster is about 0.43 mm in
primary visual cortex; next door in a secondary visual area,
it's 0.65 mm; in the sensory strip, it's 0.73 mm; and in motor
cortex of monkeys, it's 0.85 mm. Let me, for convenience, just
call this skip-spacing a generic 0.5 mm. The axon may then
continue for an identical distance and sprout another terminal
cluster, and this express train line may continue for some millimeters.

This skip-spacing is distinctly peculiar in the annals of
cortical neuroanatomy. Its function is unknown, but it certainly does make you think that regions 0.5 mm apart might
be doing the same thing on occasion—that there could be
repeating patterns of activity, in the manner of recurring patterns within wallpaper.

THE SKIP-SPACING, you may have noticed, is the same half millimeter or so as the distance between macrocolumns. Color
blobs, too, are about that far apart from one another. Yet
there's a difference.

A second superficial pyramidal neuron 0.2 mm from the
first will itself have an axon with different express stops, still
at 0.5 mm skips but each cluster landing 0.2 mm from those of
the first. In my undergraduate days, the Chicago Transit
Authority had exactly such a system of A trains and B trains,
one taking the "even" stops and the other the "odd" numbered
ones, with a few common stops for transferring between
trains. Of course, any one subway stop is sometimes stretched
out over more than a city block—and our superficial pyramidal neurons are also not located at a single point, as their dendritic tree spreads sideways from the cell body, often 0.1 mm
or more.

Contrast this to macrocolumns. So far, they've been *territories* within which there is common source of input, as if you

could draw a fence around a group of minicolumns on the basis of their all being on the same mailing list. And the blobs have an output target in common (secondary cortical areas specializing in color). So we're *not* talking macrocolumns with our sideways-running excitatory axon branches, though perhaps the skip-spacing is a cause (or effect) of the macro-columns at an adjacent level of organization. Imagine a forest where tree branches interdigitate, where each tree has a tele-phone line leaving it and contacting a distant tree, not only bypassing the intermediate ones, but leaping over the common-input fences subdividing the forest.

Sideways "recurrent" connections are common in real neural networks; lateral inhibition was the topic of two Nobel Prizes (to Georg von Békésy in 1961 and H. Keffer Hartline in 1967). It tends to sharpen up fuzzy boundaries in a spatial pattern (while they may compensate for fuzzy optics, they can also produces a few side effects, such as some of the visual illusions). But our superficial pyramidal neurons are *excitatory* to one another, suggesting that their activity could feed on itself like a spreading brushfire, unless held in check by inhibitory neurons. What's going on here? Is recurrent excita-tion why the cerebral cortex is so prone to epileptic seizures, when the inhibitory neurons are fatigued?

Furthermore, the standard skip-spacing means that a round-trip might be possible—a reverberating circuit, of the kind postulated by early neurophysiologists. Two neurons that are 0.5 mm apart may keep each other going. A neuron has a refractory period—a kind of "dead zone"—after an impulse is produced: for a millisecond or so, it is almost impossible to initiate another impulse. The travel time over that 0.5 mm is also about a millisecond, and then the synap-tic delay slows delivery by another half a millisecond—so if the connections between the two neurons were otherwise strong enough, you can imagine the second neuron's impulse getting back to the first neuron about the time it has recov-ered its ability to generate another impulse. But usually con-nection strength between neurons isn't strong enough, and usually such rapid firing cannot be kept up, even if it does get started. (In the heart, however, connection strengths between adjacent cells are indeed strong enough, and *circus re-excitation* is an important pathology when injury slows travel times.)

If the implication of cortex's standard skip-spacing isn't an impulse chasing its tail, then what is it? Probably synchronization.

IF YOU SING IN THE CHORUS, you get in sync with the others by hearing them—usually hearing yourself coming in too late or starting too early. But you, of course, are also influencing them. Even if everyone is a little hard of hearing, everyone soon gets synchronized, thanks to all that feedback.

Your position in that chorus is very much like that of a superficial pyramidal neuron in the neocortex, getting excitatory inputs from neighbors on all sides. Networks like this have been extensively studied, even if the one in superficial neocortex has not; synchronization will occur even with only small amounts of feedback (which is why I postulated that you were hard of hearing, just then). Two identical pendulums will tend to synchronize if they are adjacent, just from the air and shelf vibrations they create. Menstrual cycles are said to synchronize in women's dormitories. Though harmonic oscillators, such as the pendulums, take a while to get in sync, nonlinear systems, such as impulse production in neurons, can synchronize very quickly, even if the mutual connection strengths are relatively weak.

And what does this tendency to synchronize have to do with copying spatiotemporal patterns? Happily, it's all a matter of simple geometry, the kind that the ancient Greeks discovered while staring at the tile mosaics of their bathhouse floors (and that many of us have rediscovered in wallpaper patterns).

LET US SUPPOSE THAT A "BANANA COMMITTEE" is forming among all the superficial pyramidal neurons scattered around the primary visual cortex that respond to one feature or another of the banana you're looking at. The lines forming the outline of the banana are a particularly effective prod to those neurons that specialize in boundaries and their orientation. Then there are those blob neurons that like yellow.

Since they tend to excite one another, given that 0.5 mm skip-distance for their axon terminal clusters, there is going to be a tendency for them to synchronize—not that all impulses in the neuron I'll call Yellow One will be synchronized with those in Yellow Two, but a certain percentage will occur within a few milliseconds of one another.

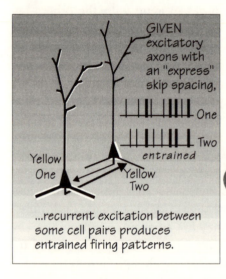

GIVEN excitatory axons with an "express" skip spacing,

One

Two

entrained

Yellow One

Yellow Two

...recurrent excitation between some cell pairs produces entrained firing patterns.

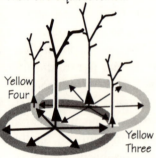

An entrained pair tends to recruit additional cells that are equidistant...

Yellow Four

Yellow Three

...and so create a TRIANGULAR ARRAY of synchronized neurons extending some distance.

Suppose now that there is another superficial pyramidal neuron, 0.5 mm equidistant from both Yellow One and Yellow Two. Perhaps it only receives a weak yellow input, so that it isn't actively firing away, signaling yellow. Now, however, Yellow Three is getting inputs from both One and Two. Furthermore, some of those inputs from One and Two—the synchronized ones—will arrive at Three's dendrites together. (They both have the same 0.5 mm travel distance.) This is exactly what hi-fi buffs call "sitting in the hot spot," equidistant from both speakers at the apex of an equilateral triangle (move even slightly to either side and the stereo illusion collapses into the nearest speaker, leaving you with mono sound). At the cortical hot spot near Three, the two synaptic inputs summate, 2 + 2 = 4 (approximately). But the distance remaining to the impulse threshold may be 10, so Three still remains silent.

Not very interesting. But these are glutamate synapses in the superficial cortical layers, so they've got NMDA channels across the synapse to let both sodium and calcium into the downstream neuron. Again, not so important—by itself.

But I temporarily omitted telling you why neurophysiologists find NMDA channels so fascinating compared with other synaptic channels: they are sensitive not only to arriving glutamate but also to the preexisting voltage across the postsynaptic membrane. Raise that voltage and the next glutamate to arrive will cause a bigger effect, sometimes twice the standard amount. This is because many of the NMDA channels are normally sitting there plugged up: there's a magnesium ion stuck in the middle of the tunnel through the membrane; increased voltage will pop it out of there—and that in turn allows formerly blocked sodium and calcium to flow into the dendrite on the next occasion when arriving glutamate opens up the gates.

The consequence of this is important: it means that synchronously arriving impulses are more effective than 2 + 2 would predict: the sum could be 6 or 8 instead (welcome to nonlinearity). *Repeated* near-synchronization of two inputs is even more effective, as they clean the magnesium plugs out of each other's channels. Pretty soon, those repeatedly synchronous inputs from Yellow One and Yellow Two might be able to trigger an impulse from Yellow Three.

Standard-distance mutual re-excitation and NMDA synaptic strength augmentation have this interesting hand-and-glove fit, all because of the tendency to synchronize. Emergent properties often come from just such combinations of the seemingly unrelated.

WE NOW HAVE THREE ACTIVE NEURONS, forming the corners of an equilateral triangle. But there might be a fourth, over on the other side of One and Two, also equidistant at 0.5 mm away. There isn't very much data yet on how many axon branches there are from a single superficial pyramidal neuron—but looking down from the top, in one dye-filled and exhaustively reconstructed superficial pyramidal neuron, showed branches in many directions. So there ought to be a doughnutlike ring of excitation, about 0.5 mm away from the neuron. Two such rings, with centers 0.5 mm apart—as from Yellow One and Two—have two intersections, just as in that plane geometry exercise about bisecting a line.

So it wouldn't be surprising if Yellow One and Yellow Two, once they got their act in sync, managed to recruit a Yellow Four as well as a Yellow Three. And there are other neurons at the hot spot of the pair formed by One and Three: perhaps a Yellow Five will join the chorus, if it already has enough other inputs to put the paired inputs within range of its threshold. As you can see, there is a tendency to form a *triangular array* of often-synchronized neurons that could extend for a few millimeters across the cortical surface.

Because one neuron can become surrounded by six others, all telling it to fire at a certain time, we have error correction: even if a neuron tries to do something different, it is forced back to the choral pattern that has become established by its insistent neighbors. That is essentially an error-correction procedure, just what the *faux* fax needs—if only the long corticocortical axon terminals did what the local ones do: fan out into patches about 0.5 mm apart rather than ending in a point.

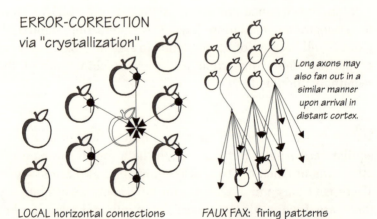

ERROR-CORRECTION
via "crystallization"

Long axons may also fan out in a similar manner upon arrival in distant cortex.

LOCAL horizontal connections in superficial layers enforce conformity by repeatedly synchronous inputs.

FAUX FAX: firing patterns are reconstituted even when only when 2 or 3 (out of 7) inputs arrive simultaneously.

And they do fan out in a patchy manner—in about the right ballpark.

THE NOTION OF "CONVERGENCE ZONES" for associative memories raises the issue of maintaining the identity of a spatiotemporal code during long-distance corticocortical messaging, such as through the corpus callosum from the left side to the right of the brain. Distortions of the spatiotemporal pattern by a lack of precise topographic mappings (axon terminations are always fanning out, not ending in a single point), or a dispersion in time (conduction velocities are not uniform), might be unimportant where the information flows in only the one direction—in that case, one arbitrary code is simply replaced by another arbitrary code in that pathway.

But because the connections between distant cortical regions are typically (six in every seven paths) reciprocal, any distortions of the original spatiotemporal firing pattern during forward transmission would need to be compensated in the reverse path, in order to maintain the characteristic spatiotemporal pattern as the local code for a sensory or motor schema. You could straighten out the distortion with an inverse transform, just as in decompressing a compressed file. Or you could fix it with the aforementioned error-correction mechanism. Or you could just live with different codes locally meaning the same thing, like names and nicknames—what's called a degenerate code, as when six different DNA triplets all code for leucine. I used to think that either alternative was more likely than an error-correction scheme, but then I didn't realize how simply error correction could emerge from the crystallization that ought to accompany recurrent excitation and synchrony-sensitive NMDA channels.

Imagine an optical fiber array connecting one cortical area with its homologous one on the other side. Real optical fiber bundles subdivide an image into dots, then faithfully pipe each dot a long distance so that, looking at the end of the fiber bundle, you see a pattern of lighted dots identical to that at the front end.

An axon is not like a light pipe because of all the "sprouts" at each end. It doesn't end in a point: a single axon fans out into many terminals, spreading over macrocolumn dimensions. Bundles of real axons also aren't like a coherent fiber-optic bundle, where neighbors remain faithful neighbors; real axons can get intertwined with one another, so that a dot goes astray and ends up displaced at the other end. Real axons also vary somewhat in conduction velocity: impulses that started out together may arrive at different times, distorting the spatiotemporal pattern.

But the local error-correction property suggests that none of this might matter very much, at the far end of a corticocortical bundle. What's being sent is a *redundant* spatiotemporal pattern, thanks to those triangular arrays on the originating end. Each point on the distant end might get an input from a dead-on-target axon, plus up to six inputs from neighbors 0.5 mm away back home; yes, some get lost, and some impulses arrive too late, but a receiving neuron preferentially pays attention to the repeatedly synchronous inputs, and perhaps only a few of them are needed to reproduce the firing pattern of the originating point, effectively ignoring the stragglers and the wanderers.

Once a small region of spatiotemporal pattern is re-formed again on the distant end, it can expand to clone a larger territory, just as explained earlier. So synchronized triangular arrays make it possible for sloppy wiring to send spatiotemporal patterns over long distances in the cortex—provided you start with a dozen or so spatial repeats of the spatiotemporal pattern and end with a sufficient territory of the same pattern on the far end.

How big might an array become? It might be confined to its original Brodmann area, if the skip-spacing changed at the boundary. For example, in primary visual cortex, the skip-spacing in monkeys is 0.43 mm, and next door in the secondary visual area it's 0.65 mm; recruiting across the boundary might not work, but that's an empirical question—we'll just have to see. And recruiting more neurons into the triangular array requires candidates that are already mildly interested in the banana.

So the triangular array of Yellows might not be too much larger than the part of the visual cortex receiving the image of the yellow banana. The neurons sensitive to line orientation might have been doing the same thing, too: several getting in sync, recruiting a chorus of the predisposed, and so forming another 0.5 mm triangular array centered elsewhere. For each separately detected feature of the banana, there would be a different triangular array—and not necessarily extending the same distances across the cortex. Looking down on the flattened cortex (and assuming that a minicolumn lights up when an impulse fires), we would see a lot of flickering lights.

If we restricted our field of view to a 0.5 mm circle, we would be unlikely to see much synchrony, just one of the Yellows firing a few times a second, one of the Lines firing a dozen times a second, and so on. But if we broadened our field of view to several millimeters, we would see a half-dozen spots lighting up at once, then another group lighting up. Each specialty has its own triangular array; taken together, the various arrays constitute a Banana Committee.

Note that the original committee of Yellows and Lines might have been larger than 0.5 mm across, back before recruitment began to fill in things. Even if the original committee was scattered over a few millimeters, the triangular arrays serve to create a unit pattern that is much smaller (and potentially easier to re-create, when recalling the pattern). We have, in effect, compacted the code into a smaller space than it originally occupied, as well as making redundant copies. That has some interesting implications.

THIS IS A SPATIOTEMPORAL PATTERN having something to do with a banana's representation, but is it the *cerebral code* for banana? I'd call that the smallest such pattern that didn't omit anything important—the elementary pattern from which the triangular arrays of Lines and Yellow could be re-created.

If we zoom in, shrinking our field of view of the flickering minicolumns, what area will it cover at the point where we can no longer find synchronized minicolumns? Yes, it's about 0.5 mm, but it isn't a 0.5 mm circle—it is a hexagon that is 0.5 mm across between parallel faces. This is a simple matter of geometry: corresponding points (say, the upper right corners) of hexagonal tiles form triangular arrays. Anything larger than that hexagon will start including some redundant points that are represented by another of their triangular array (and we'd sometimes see two synchronized points in our restricted view of view).

The elementary pattern wouldn't usually fill the hexagon (I imagine it as a dozen minicolumns active, out of a hundred or more in the hexagon—but the rest have to stay silent in order not to fog the pattern). We wouldn't be able to see the boundaries outlined—so that we wouldn't see a honeycomb when we looked down on the cortical surface while a territory was being cloned. Indeed, when wallpaper designers create a repeating pattern, they often make sure that the pattern unit's boundary cannot be easily detected, so that the overall pattern will appear seamless. Though the triangular arrays do the recruitment and create the compact pattern, it is as if hexagons were being cloned.

The triangular synchronicity doesn't necessarily last for very long—it's an ephemeral form of organization, and it might be wiped out during certain phases of an EEG rhythm associated with decreases in cortical excitability. If we want to re-create a spatiotemporal pattern that has died out, we could get it started from within two adjacent hexagons—indeed, from *any* two adjacent hexagons that the extended banana mosaic covered originally. It wouldn't have to be the original pairs. The memory trace—the essential bumps and ruts for resurrecting the spatiotemporal pattern—could be as small as the circuitry in two adjacent hexagons.

So repeated copying of the minimal pattern could colonize a region, in much the same way that a crystal grows or wallpaper repeats an elementary pattern. If the melody recurred enough times before it stopped, LTP might linger in such a way that the spatiotemporal pattern was easily restarted, at one place or another.

If the spatial pattern was relatively sparse, several cerebral codes (say, the ones for Apple and Tangerine) could be superimposed to give you a category, such as Fruit. If you tried superimposing several letters from a dot-matrix printer, you'd get a black mess. But if the matrix is sparsely filled, you can probably recover the individual members, because they each produce such distinctive spatiotemporal patterns. So this type of code could also be handy for forming categories that could be decomposed into examples, just as superimposed melodies can often be heard individually. Thanks to the telecopying aspect, you could form multimodal categories—such as all of the connotations of *comb.*

My friend Don Michael suggests that meditation might correspond to creating, via a mantra, a large mosaic of a nonsense code, one without significant resonances or associations. If you maintained it long enough to wipe the slate clean of cares and preoccupations, allowing those short-term ruts to fade, it might give you a fresh start in accessing long-term memory ruts without getting hung up on short-term concerns.

> *[Meditation's] exquisite state of unconcerned immersion in oneself is not, unfortunately, of long duration. It is liable to be disturbed from inside. As though sprung from nowhere, moods, feelings, desires, worries and even thoughts incontinently rise up, in a meaningless jumble, and the more far-fetched and preposterous they are, and the less they have to do with that on which one has fixed one's consciousness, the more tenaciously they hang on. . . . The only successful way of rendering this disturbance inoperative is to keep on breathing, quietly and unconcernedly, to enter into friendly relations with whatever appears on the scene, to accustom oneself to it, to look at it equably and at last grow weary of looking.*
>
> EUGEN HERRIGEL, *Zen in the Art of Archery*, 1953

THERE ARE SOME ATTRACTIVE FEATURES to what emerges from this analysis of the superficial pyramidal neurons: Donald Hebb would have loved it, because it shows how some of the most puzzling features of short- and long-term memory might be explained with cell assemblies (the memory trace is stored in a distributed way, with no one site crucial for its recall, and so forth). The gestalt psychologists would have liked the way that it makes possible the comparison of figure and ground by the triangular arrays potentially extending beyond the object boundaries, a spatiotemporal pattern forming that represents the figure-ground *combination*, rather than just one or the other.

And I like to think that Charles Darwin and William James would have liked the idea that mental life involves copying competitions biased by a multifaceted environment. Sigmund Freud might have been intrigued with the mechanism it suggests for how subconscious associations could occasionally pop into the foreground of consciousness.

While I think that divergent thinking is the most important application of the neocortical Darwin Machine, let me first illustrate how it might work with a convergent thinking problem. Suppose that something whizzes past you and disappears under a chair. You thought it was round, and maybe orange or yellow, but it was moving very quickly, and now it's out of sight, so you can't get a second look. What was it? How do you guess, when the answer isn't obvious? Your process first needs to find some candidates, then it needs to compare them for reasonableness.

Happily, cloning competitions can do that. There's a tentative cerebral code for the object, formed by all the feature detectors that it activated: color, shape, motion, and maybe the sound of it bouncing on the floor. This spatiotemporal pattern starts making clones of itself, in a manner of speaking.

Whether it can set up a clone next door depends on the resonances next door, those bumps in the road provided by the pattern of synaptic strengths and by whatever else is going on in the adjacent cortex. If you'd seen such an object many times before, there might be a perfect resonance—but you haven't. Still, the tentative cerebral code has specialty components of Round, Yellow, Fast. Tennis balls have such attributes, and you have a good tennis-ball resonance, so the adjacent area pops into the melody for Tennis Ball (a nice feature of attractors is that a near fit can be captured and transformed to the characteristic pattern). Cloning with poor resonances leads to dropouts of some components, so perhaps your Tangerine resonance captures a variant in another patch of cortex despite the color not being quite right.

WHAT ABOUT CLONING COMPETITIONS? Here we have Unknown, Tennis Ball, and Tangerine cerebral codes cloning away. Perhaps Apple pops out as well: if you saw someone eating an apple a few minutes ago, there would be temporary ruts for Apple, because of the NMDA synapses that were strengthened in that pattern. But then Apple is overrun by the Tangerine pattern, which is cloning away. Over on the other side of Unknown's current territory, Tennis Ball is doing quite well and eventually it overrides and replaces Unknown, even encroaching on Tangerine's territory. At about this time, you say, "I think that was a tennis ball," because there were finally enough clones in the Tennis Ball chorus to get a coherent message through to your left-lateral language cortex, over the corticocortical pathways from the occipital lobe to the temporal lobe.

Something else happens now: a new spatiotemporal pattern starts cloning through the work space; this time, you see

Darwin Machine handles ambiguity, finding candidates and making decision

SENSORY BUFFER

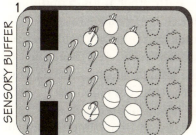

Fence of inhibition prevents error correction, allows variants at "gate."

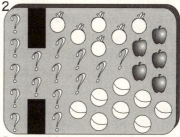

Three candidates have been found via variants being captured by an attractor.

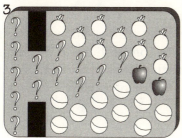

Competition ensues, skewed by extrinsic biases and fading traces.

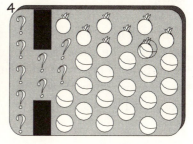

Critical mass: "It was a tennis ball!"

something very familiar (the chair) and a critical chorus of Chair is quickly established without any real competition, because the sensory spatiotemporal pattern hits instantly on a resonance before any variants have time to get going. The NMDA synapses used in the Tennis Ball and Tangerine patterns are still jazzed up, however, and for another five minutes it will be easier than usual to re-create either of these spatiotemporal patterns in the parts of the work space that they last occupied. Perhaps Tangerine continues to clone and make mistakes, hitting upon the Orange Fruit resonance—so that a minute later, you wonder if you were wrong about that tennis ball.

That's how it could happen—how I imagine that our subconscious processes sometimes come up with someone's name a half hour too late. The pattern resonances are not unlike how we imagine locomotion to work in the spinal cord: there's a connectivity—all those synaptic strengths between the various neurons—and, given certain initial conditions, you can pop into the resonance for the spatiotemporal pattern that implements Walk. With other initial conditions, you pop instead into Jog, Lope, Run, or Hopscotch.

In the sensory cortex, you may pop into Orange or Tangerine even when you see fruit that is neither. As I mentioned in chapter 5, categories are why the Japanese have so much trouble with English L and R sounds: both are captured by their mental category for a particular Japanese phoneme. Reality is quickly replaced by mental models. As Henry David Thoreau said, "We hear and apprehend only what we already half know."

The cortex is in the business of quickly learning new patterns, whether sensory or movement, and creating variations on them. The variations allow for competitions to determine what pattern best resonates with the connectivities, and these in turn are often biased by a number of sensory inputs and emotional drives.

RELATIONSHIPS, TOO, CAN BE CODED by spatiotemporal patterns— just as sensory or movement schemas are. Just combine codes to make a new arbitrary pattern, in the same way that a left-hand rhythm can be superimposed on a right-hand melody.

The *lingua ex machina* of chapter 5 offered some specific examples of what fancy relationships (as in a sentence) might involve—all those obligatory and optional roles. Those obligatory arguments of a verb such as *give* are about relationships, and cognitive dissonance results when an obligatory role goes unfilled (as, alas, advertising agencies have discovered; *Give Him* forces you to read the billboard again to see what you missed, and thereby remember the ad better).

So, is a sentence simply one big spatiotemporal pattern, cloning away in competition with other sentence codes? Yes, but not always. We don't require copying competitions in order to make a decision; simple rating schemes ought to suffice, if nothing particularly new is involved. Recall the cormorant of chapter 2: rating schemes will do for its decision making, because the choices (swim, dive, dry wings, fly away, look around a little longer) are already well shaped by evolution over the generations. Copyable schemas aren't everything, once you get close enough to standard meanings.

THE SUPERFICIAL CORTICAL LAYERS in many primates have the standard skip-wiring that predicts the ephemeral triangular arrays. It is not known how often any animal uses this wiring for cloning wallpaperlike hexagonal patterns; perhaps it only happens briefly, during prenatal development—as a sort of test pattern that guides use-dependent connections—and never occurs again. Or perhaps some areas of cortex are committed to full-time specialization and never clone such ephemeral patterns, while other areas often support sideways copying and become erasable workspaces for darwinian shaping-up processes. Since clones of movement commands would be particularly useful for throwing—they can reduce timing jitter—perhaps there was some natural selection for big work spaces in the hominid evolution of throwing accuracy. They're all empirical questions. Once we have improved the resolution of our recording techniques, we'll have to see where hexagonal cloning lies on the spectrum of possibilities.

But something very close to such cloning competitions is needed to satisfy the essentials for the Darwin Machine—

that's the real reason why I've led the reader through this cortical maze. Here, at least, we have (1) a distinctive pattern; (2) copying; (3) variation; (4) possible competitions for work spaces; (5) multifaceted environments (both current and memorized) to bias the competition; and (6) a next generation more likely to have variants established from the clones with the biggest territories (big territories have more perimeter, which is where variants can escape error-correction tendencies and get started cloning their new pattern).

In a longer book about the neocortical Darwin Machine itself (*The Cerebral Code*), I'll explain all about the spice and speed that you'd get from cerebral analogues of sex, islands, and climate change. And speed we need, if a darwinian process in the brain is to work fast enough to provide our guessing-right intelligence.

WE KEEP TRYING TO CARVE UP THE CEREBRAL CORTEX into specialized "expert" modules. It's a good research strategy to look for specialization, but I don't take it seriously as an overview of how the association cortex works. We need some erasable work spaces, and we need to be able to recruit helpers for difficult tasks. That suggests that any "expert" modules are also generalists—as when a neurosurgeon acts as a paramedic in an emergency. One of the things I like about the ephemeral hexagonal mosaic is that it suggests a resolution of the expert-generalist dilemmas: even a cortical area with "expert" long-term ruts could serve as a work space, using overlaid short-term ruts to bias competitions.

Such a mosaic also suggests a way that subconscious thoughts could meander and occasionally pop some relevant fact from the past into your stream of consciousness. Best of all, because variants themselves can clone their way to temporary success, the patchwork quilt is creative—it can be shaped up from humble beginnings into something of quality. Even higher forms of relationships, such as metaphor, seem likely to arise, because the cerebral codes are arbitrary and capable of forming new combinations. Who knows—perhaps by now you've even acquired a cerebral code for Umberto Eco's Mac-PC analogy.

THE SYNCHRONIZED TRIANGULAR ARRAYS with such interesting implications for darwinian copying competitions turn out to have
implications for fancy language as well, potentially giving
intelligence a boost from another direction.

There is a considerable step up from protolanguage (page
71) to our full-fledged syntactic language, yet linguistics
researchers doubt that intermediate forms exist. Even when it
has ample vocabulary, protolanguage has very little structure,
relying mostly on simple contextual associations between a
few words to convey the message. Adding structure makes a
big difference.

A brain mechanism for recursive embedding (such as sentences within sentences: *I think I saw him leave to go home*) is
considered essential for Universal Grammar. Among the linguists' other desiderata are mechanisms for long-range dependencies, including binding of pronouns to their referents.
Such binding requires longer-than-local links; recursive
embedding, moreover, requires structuring a hierarchy of
them. Nonadjacent areas of cerebral cortex are likely to be
involved in many attempted associations, given what we
know about *comb's* visual connotations being stored near
visual cortex, its auditory aspects near auditory areas, and so
forth.

Yet corticocortical axon bundles are considerably worse
than the incoherent fiber optic bundles, where neighbors fail
to remain neighbors. Point-to-point mappings are also likely
to be lost as each axon's terminals fan out, not unlike the
spread of a flashlight beam. Despite incoherence from both
jumble and smear, some of the distorted patterns can presumably, with experience, be recognized at the far end, using
cluster-analysis-like mechanisms analogous to those of categorical perception. This ought to allow the conveyance of
well-practiced special cases, analogous to the mariners' signal
flags—though perhaps only a few at a time, thereby limiting
the possible novel associations that could be conveyed
between cortical areas. Embedding would be restricted to
stock phrases. This incoherent level of corticocortical capabil-
ity ought to be able to handle protolanguage.

But the error-correction mechanism (page 130) offers the
possibility of sending arbitrary spatiotemporal patterns down

the corticocortical bundle—and succeeding on the first try, so that one is no longer limited to the spatially and temporally distorted patterns that have been recognized by the target cortex as meaningful special cases. Such corticocortical coherence would mean that novel associations could be conveyed. Furthermore, the same spatiotemporal firing pattern would now be shared by both the source and the target area; the target cortex could send it back with similar error correction and have it automatically recognized in the source cortex, with no need to tune up to a doubly distorted version and then construct an equivalence to the original spatiotemporal firing pattern.

Back projections using the same code mean that you can have a distributed choir, distant chorus members contributing to keeping its membership above a critical size. A back-projected song might not need to be fully featured to help out with the chorus. It could be more like that sing-along technique in which a single voice monotonically prompts the next verse and the audience repeats it with musical elaborations. Back projections also provide an audit trail that can resolve ambiguity. ("Who said X? Sing it again, the whole thing!") With links that can maintain sentence structure, embedding becomes possible: no longer is there a danger that the mental model of the eight-word amalgamation *the tall blond man with one black shoe* will be scrambled into *a blond black man with one tall shoe.*

Corticocortical precision per se is thus one candidate for the big step up from protolanguage to Language (though you still need lots of little rules at the level of argument structure). Indeed, the transition to arbitrary code conveyance could have implemented two major innovations of Universal Grammar—embedding and long-range links—in one step. So we now have several candidates, Darwin Machines and coherent corticocorticals, for what might have boosted intelligence and language, enabling the infrequently innovating *Homo erectus* cultures to evolve, about 250,000 years ago, into the constantly changing cultures of *Homo sapiens.*

*At the conclusion of all our studies we must try
once again to experience the human soul as soul,
and not just as a buzz of bioelectricity; the
human will as will, and not just a surge of
hormones; the human heart not as a fibrous,
sticky pump, but as the metaphoric organ of
understanding. We need not believe in them as
metaphysical entities—they are as real as the
flesh and blood they are made of. But we must
believe in them as entities; not as analyzed
fragments, but as wholes made real by our
contemplation of them, by the words we use to
talk of them, by the way we have transmuted
them to speech. We must stand in awe of them as
unassailable, even though they are dissected
before our eyes.*

MELVIN KONNER, 1991

....

CHAPTER 8

PROSPECTS FOR A
SUPERHUMAN INTELLIGENCE

*Of course, if my "self" is a mere bundle of
instincts of known number and exact dimension,
then let me tie the bundle up neatly and make
the best of it; but if this elusive personality, with
its queer and satisfying aspirations and relapses
and struggles and touches of the eternal, is not
just a machine with wheels that get out of order
and a definitive maximum horsepower, but a
living thing infinitely variable, constantly
readjusting itself to circumstances, capable of
incalculable achievement or of pathetic
meanness, in some sense master of its fate; if its
freedom is not an illusion, and its possibility of
spiritual experience not a lie, then we must not
allow ourselves to fall back into the old error of
the mechanistic materialist.*
                CHARLES E. RAVEN, *The Creator Spirit*, 1928

WE HAVE A LIFE OF THE MIND, and it is because of the dynamic
darwinism of our mental lives that we can invent—and daily
reinvent—ourselves. That life of the mind, a muddle at the
beginning of this book, perhaps can now be imagined as a dar-

winian process—a high-level one, up near the top of those levels of stratified stability—that is capable of implementing Charles Raven's sense of self. Such depth and versatility could emerge from cerebral codes cloning away, competing for territory with other cerebral codes, and spinning out new variations.

It's not a computer, at least not in our usual sense of a reliable machine that can faithfully repeat its actions. For most people, it's something new in the mechanistic realm, utterly without good analogies—except for the other known darwinian processes. But you can get a feeling for what it's like: looking down on the (virtually flattened) surface of the cortex would be like seeing a mosaic—a dynamic patchwork quilt, with the "patches" never at rest. On closer inspection, each patch would appear like a wallpaper pattern that repeated, but each unit pattern would be dynamic, a twinkling spatiotemporal pattern, rather than the traditional static one. The boundaries between adjacent patches of the quilt would sometimes be stable, sometimes moving, like a battlefront. Sometimes the unit patterns would fade from an area, the triangular arrays no longer synchronizing homologous points—and another unit pattern, unopposed, might quickly colonize the disorganized territory.

The current winner of that copying competition, the one with the biggest chorus vying for the attention of the output pathways, looks like a good candidate for what we term consciousness. Our shifting focus could be another clone coming to the fore. Our subconscious could be the other active patterns not currently dominant. No particular area in cortex is the "center of consciousness" for very long before another takes over.

The shifting mosaics also seem to provide a good candidate for intelligence. Among the spatiotemporal patterns that they shape up are the commands for novel movements. The evolving mosaics can discover new order à la Horace Barlow, since spatiotemporal patterns can vary to find new resonances. The mosaics can simulate actions in the real world à la Kenneth Craik, since the cerebral code for a movement schema can be judged against the resonances of long-term memories and the current sensory inputs. They have Jean

Piaget's feature of handling situations in which it isn't obvious what to do next.

And the mosaics have the open-ended aspect of our mental lives—as when we invent new levels of complexity, like crossword puzzles, or (as can be the case with poems) compound symbols to embody new levels of meaning. Because the cerebral codes can represent not just sensory and movement schemas but also ideas, we can imagine metaphors of quality emerging, can imagine how Coleridge's "willing suspension of disbelief" takes place when we enter into an imaginary realm of fiction.

Cerebral codes and darwinian processes were what I had in mind back at the beginning of this book, when I suggested that by its end the reader might be able to imagine a process that could result in consciousness and could operate fast enough to constitute a quick intelligence, good at guessing. This last chapter is about the implications of augmenting our brains and creating artificial approximations. But let me begin with a sideways glance at competing styles of explanation.

THE GOLD STANDARD OF EXPLANATION—the one to which all the sciences aspire (though sometimes inappropriately)—is abstract and mathematical. It is surely impressive when someone can unfold, from a set of abstract definitions and axioms, a forward-leaping chain of inferences. From Plato's ideal, both Descartes and Kant tried to understand how the mind could operate mathematically. We finally seem on the threshold of answering some such questions.

But there have long been challenges to the whole scientific enterprise—challenges that will come strongly into play once again, as science tries to explain the human mind. The mystic's and irrationalist's visions of truth spring from illumination, not deduction; the truths of science are seen by them as second-rate and impatient, compared to those achieved by pure contemplation. A second challenge is from dogma; Galileo got into trouble not over his astronomy but because his scientific methods of constant challenge and revision threatened the very concept of revealed truth that religions used to make their world view seem everlasting and internally coherent. Then there is what the literary critic George Steiner calls the challenge from "romantic existential polemic"—Nietzsche's preference for instinctive wisdom over sterile deduction, for instance, or Blake's critique of Newton's optics of the rainbow. A fourth line of attack sees ulterior motives everywhere, or claims that truth is relative to political viewpoints.

These are fundamentally challenges from outside the scientific tradition; their modern-day adherents will surely seize upon our everyday scientific confusions and try to exploit them, in the manner of the fundamentalist Christian attack on evolutionary biology itself. Such styles of explanation have long competed with science, with a few short-term wins (such as La Mettrie's exile) and many long-term losses. Threads from all four can be found today in the movements founded by the dropouts from the age of reason.

So we must try to be clear about our scientific explanations and not create false oppositions—like the supposed conflict between the principles of evolution by genetic mutations and natural selection, a needless confusion that lasted for decades until resolved in the 1940s by the Modern Synthesis. We must avoid using mathematical concepts to dazzle rather than enlighten; we must watch out for "proofs by want of imagination," as when we conclude, out of arrogance or impatience, that there are no other alternatives to the answers we have found. When it comes to the brain, in particular, we must be careful to pitch our theories at the right level of mechanistic explanation.

> *Accordingly, the neuron level of description that provides the currently fashionable picture of the brain and mind is a mere* shadow *of the deeper level of cytoskeletal action—and it is at this deeper level where we must seek the physical basis of* mind!
> ROGER PENROSE, *Shadows of the Mind*, 1994

I'M SURE SOME CONSCIOUSNESS PHYSICIST or ecclesiastical neuroscientist will say, despite all the prior chapters, that a ghost in the machine is still necessary, leaping over those dozen intermediate levels of stratified stability to provide a guiding role for enigmatic quantum mechanics, down there in the micro-tubules of the neuron's cytoskeleton, where some immaterial spirit can interface with the brain's biological machinery. Actually, such theorists usually avoid the word "spirit" and say something about quantum fields. I'll be happy to compromise on "mystery" using Dan Dennett's definition: a phenomenon that people don't know how to think about. All that the consciousness physicists have accomplished is the replacement of one mystery by another; so far, there are no parts and pieces of their explanations, the combinations of which can explain other things.

And even if they improve on their combinations, any effects from synchronized microtubules would only provide us with another candidate for the unitary nature of our conscious experience—one that will have to compete in mechanistic detail with explanations at other levels, and which will have to compete with them for sheer coverage. The darwinian process, thus far, seems to have the right parts and pieces to explain the successes and malfunctions of important aspects of consciousness.

I think we'll continue to see those tiresome debates in which one philosopher tries to hog-tie another philosopher (or at least paint him into a corner, brick him up with a wall of words) over the issue of whether a machine can ever truly understand anything, whether they will ever be able to have our kind of consciousness. Unfortunately, even if all scientists and philosophers agreed about how mind arises from brain, the complexity of the subject would still cause most people to abstract that complexity, using some simpler-to-imagine concept such as "spirit." And perhaps to feel like the book reviewer who said (perhaps rhetorically), "Is the digital computer merely a simpler version of the human brain, as many theorists contend? If in fact it is, the implications are scary."

Scary? Personally, I find ignorance scary. It has a substantial track record, what with demonic possession "explaining" mental illness, and all those witch trials and inquisitions. We badly need a metaphor more useful than a quantum-mechanical mystery; we need a metaphor that successfully bridges the gap between our perceived mental life and the neural mechanisms responsible for it.

So far, we've actually needed two metaphors: a top-down metaphor that maps thoughts onto ensembles of neurons, and a bottom-up metaphor that accounts for how ideas emerge from those apparently chaotic neuron ensembles. But the neocortical Darwin Machine may well do for both metaphors—if it really is the creative mechanism within.

THE NEOCORTICAL DARWIN MACHINE THEORY seems to me to be at the right level of explanation; it's not down in the synapse or cytoskeleton but up at the level of dynamics involving tens of thousands of neurons, generating the spatiotemporal patterns that are the precursors of movement—of behavior in the world outside the brain. Moreover, the theory is consistent with a lot of phenomena from a century of brain research, and it's testable (with some improvement in the spatial and temporal resolution of brain imaging or microelectrode arrays).

The darwinian process at its core is, at least among biologists, widely understood as a creative mechanism. We've had well over a century to realize just how powerful such copying competitions can be, when it comes to shaping up quality from random variations on a timescale of millennia. In recent decades, we've been able to see the same process operating on the timescale of days and weeks, as the immune response creates a better-fitting antibody. That this neocortical Darwin Machine can operate in milliseconds to minutes is only another change in scale; we should be able to carry over our understanding of what the darwinian process can accomplish from evolutionary biology and immunology to the timescale of thought and action.

It seems to me that the adoption of the William James viewpoint about our mental life is long overdue. But many people, including scientists, still hold to a cardboard view of darwinism as mere selective survival (Darwin, alas, contributed to the confusion by naming his theory for only the fifth of the six essentials, natural selection). What I hope I have done in this book is to pull together all of the essentials, as well as the accelerating aspects, of a darwinian process, and then describe a specific neural mechanism that could implement such a process in primate neocortex. As mechanism rather than improved metaphor, the best thing going for my neocortical Darwin Machine at this point is that the cortical neuroanatomy and the entrained oscillators principles provide a nice fit to those six essentials of a darwinian process and the accelerating factors.

Whether this is the most important process going on in the brain, or whether another process dominates consciousness and guessing, is hard to tell; there might be one without antecedents in biology or computer science—one we cannot yet imagine without first discovering some intermediate metaphors. Indeed, I suspect that the process of "managing" the cloning competitions in order to avoid psychosis or stagnation is going to require its own metalevel of description. (I'm not thinking of a manager in the usual sense of the term but the way that global weather patterns are strongly influenced by jet streams or El Niño.) In psychological terminology, such management might be something like Raven's "elusive personality, with its queer and satisfying aspirations and relapses and struggles."

Composite cerebral codes, shaped up by darwinian copying competitions, could explain much of our mental lives. Copying competitions suggest why we humans can get away with many more novel behaviors than other animals (we have off-line evolution of nonstandard movement plans). It suggests how we can engage in analogical reasoning (relationships themselves can have codes that can compete). Because cerebral codes can be formed from pieces, you can imagine a unicorn and form a memory of it (bumps and ruts can reactivate the spatiotemporal code for unicorn). Best of all, a darwinian process provides a machine for metaphor: you can code relationships between relationships and shape them up into something of quality.

SUCH AN EXPLANATION for intelligent consciousness gives us some insight into metaphor and operations in an imaginary realm. And it ought to tell us the kinships between thought and other mental operations. In the case of my proposed explanation, the ballistic movements and music seem intimately related to thought and language. We've already seen that the emphasis on novel sequences allows for nonlanguage natural selection that benefits language (and vice versa). Those overlaps between oral-facial sequencing and hand-arm sequencing (the apraxic aphasics) suggest that both are using the same neural machinery.

The important secondary use of the neocortical Darwin Machine would be for prospective movements other than the ballistic ones: planning on the timescale of seconds, hours, days, careers. It allows for trying out combinations, judging what's wrong with them, refining them, and so forth. Individuals who are good at this are known as intelligent.

ANY EXPLANATION OF INTELLIGENCE also ought to give us some insight into other paths to intelligence than the ones followed by life on earth: it ought, in short, to have implications for artificial intelligence (AI), for augmenting animal and human intelligence, and perhaps for finding signals from exotic intelligences. Not much can yet be said on the "intelligence elsewhere" subject, but let me suggest an ethological perspective that may also help us think about AI and augmented intelligence.

An intelligence freed from the necessity of finding food and avoiding predators might (like AI) not need to move—and so such an intelligence might well lack the what-happens-next orientation of animal intelligence. We solve movement problems, and only later, in both phylogeny and ontogeny, we graduate to the pondering of more abstract problems, acting to preempt the future by guessing what lies ahead.

There may be other ways in which high intelligence can be achieved, but up-from-movement is the paradigm we know about. It is, curiously, seldom mentioned in the literature of psychology or artificial intelligence. Though there is a long intellectual thread in brain research that emphasizes up-from-movement, it is far more common to see discussions of cognitive function that emphasize a passive observer who intellectually analyzes the sensory world. Contemplation of the world still dominates most approaches to the mind, and—by itself—can be thoroughly misleading. The *exploration* of the person's world, with its constant guessing and intermittent decisions about what to do next, must be included in the way we intellectually frame the issues.

It is difficult to estimate how often high intelligence might emerge in evolutionary systems—both here on earth and elsewhere in the universe. The main limitation, which makes most speculations meaningless, is our present ignorance about how dead ends in nature are overcome: it's easy to get trapped in an equilibrium, stuck in a rut. And then there's that continuity requirement: that, at each step along the way, the species remains stable enough not to self-destruct and competitive enough not to lose out to a streamlined specialist.

Lists of intelligence attributes can, if carried far enough, be little better than stand-ins for giving a human IQ test to the other species (or computer). But we now can say something about what kinds of physiological mechanisms would aid a brain in guessing right and discovering new order.

WE COULD ASSESS PROMISING SPECIES (or artificial creations, or augmentation schemes) by counting how many building blocks of intelligence each had managed to assemble, and the number of stumbling blocks each had managed to avoid. My current assessment list would emphasize:

- A wide repertoire of movements, concepts such as words, and other tools. But even with a large vocabulary from cultural sharing over a long lifespan, high intelligence still needs additional elements in order to make novel combinations of quality.
- A tolerance for creative confusion, which would allow an individual to occasionally escape old categories and create new ones.
- More than a half-dozen simultaneous work spaces ("windows") per individual—enough so that you can pick and choose between analogies but not so many as to obviate the tendency to chunk and thereby create new vocabulary.
- Ways of establishing new relationships between the concepts in those work spaces—relations fancier than the *is-a* and *is-larger-than*, which many animals can grasp. Treelike relationships seem particularly important for our kind of

linguistic structures. Our ability to compare two relation-ships (analogy) enables operations in a metaphorical space.

- The ability to shape up off-line before acting in the real world—a shaping-up that somehow incorporated the six darwinian essentials (*patterns* that *copy*, *vary*, and *compete* judged by multifaceted *environments*, with the more successful patterns providing the center for the next round of variants) and some accelerating factors (equivalents of *recombination, climate change, islands*), with shortcuts so that the darwinian process can operate at the level of ideas rather than movements.
- The ability to formulate long-term strategies as well as short-term tactics, making intermediate moves that help set the stage for a future feat. Evolving agendas, and moni-toring their progress, helps even more.

Chimps and bonobos may be missing a few elements but they've got more of them than the present generation of AI programs.

Another implication of my darwinian theory is that, even with all the elements, we would expect considerable variation in intelligence because of individual differences in imple-menting shortcuts, in finding the appropriate level of abstrac-tion when using analogies, in processing speed, and in perse-verance (more is not always better, as when boredom allows better variants a chance to develop).

WHY AREN'T THERE MORE SPECIES with complex mental states? There is, of course, a fantasy nourished by the comic strips that attributes silent wisdom even to insects. But the apes would be the terror of Africa if they had even a tenth of our plan-ahead mental states.

I suspect that the reason there aren't more highly intelligent species is that there's a hump to get over. And it's not just a Rubicon of brain size, or a body image that permits you to imi-tate others, or a dozen other beyond-the-apes improvements seen in the hominids. *A little intelligence can be a dangerous thing*—whether it be exotic, artificial, or human. A beyond-the-apes intelligence must constantly navigate between twin hazards, just as the ancient mariners had to cope with a rock named Scylla and a whirlpool named Charybdis. The turbulence of dangerous innovation is the more obvious hazard.

> *"Well, in* our *country," said Alice, still panting a little, "you'd generally get to somewhere else—if you ran very fast for a long time, as we've been doing."*
> *"A slow sort of country!" said the [Red] Queen. "Now,* here, *you see, it takes all the* running *you* can *do, to keep in the same place. If you want to get somewhere else, you must run at least twice as fast as that!"*
> LEWIS CARROLL, *Through the Looking Glass*, 1871

The peril posed by the rock is more subtle: business-as-usual conservatism ignores what the Red Queen explained to Alice about running to stay in the same place. For example, when you're running rapids in a small boat, the way you usually get pushed against a hard rock is when you fail to maintain your speed in the main channel. Intelligence, too, is in a race with its own by-products.

Foresight is our special form of running, essential for the intelligent stewardship that the evolutionary biologist Stephen Jay Gould warns is needed for longer-term survival: "We have become, by the power of a glorious evolutionary accident called intelligence, the stewards of life's continuity on earth. We did not ask for this role, but we cannot abjure it. We may not be suited to it, but here we are."

SPEAKING OF OTHER INTELLIGENT SPECIES, what about the ones we might create ourselves? A human mind embedded *in silico*, a copy of the detailed structure of one individual's brain, is a possibility which has received some attention.

I suspect that such an "immortality machine"—the downloading of an individual's brain to a workalike computer—is unlikely to function well. Even if we neuroscientists should eventually solve the readout problem, as some physicists and computer scientists blithely assume can be done, I think that dementia, psychosis, and seizures are all too likely, unless the workalike circuits are well tuned (and stay that way). Just think of the human beings who suffer from obsessions and compulsions: "Stuck in an endless loop" takes on new meaning when the asylum is timeless, no longer limited by the human life span. Who wants to gamble on that kind of Hell?

Far better, I think, to recognize the essential nature of copying across successive generations, both of genes and memes. Richard Dawkins saw these copying relations clearly in *The Selfish Gene*, as did my friend, the futurist Thomas F. Mandel, in addressing his cyberspace friends while coping with his increasingly dim prospects of surviving lung cancer:

> I had another motive in opening this topic, to tell the truth, one that winds its way through almost everything I've done online in the five months since my cancer was diagnosed.
>
> I figured that, like everyone else, my physical self wasn't going to survive forever and I guess I was going to have less time than actuarials allocate us. But if I could reach out and touch everyone I knew on-line . . . I could toss out bits and pieces of my virtual self and the memes that make up Tom Mandel, and then when my body died, I wouldn't really have to leave. . . . Large chunks of me would also be here, part of this new space.
>
> Not an original idea, but what the hell, worth the try, and maybe one day someone can reconstruct all of the pieces in some sort of mandelbot and I can be arrogant and obstinate and affectionate and compassionate and everything else that you all seem to feel I am.

THE AD-HOC SCHEMES OF AI might also produce intelligent robots. But I think that with the aid of principles seen in neuroscience, we can build a computer that talks like a human, is as endearing as our pets, thinks in metaphor, and manages multiple levels of abstraction.

The first-order human workalike would, at a minimum, reason, categorize, and understand speech. I think that even the first-order workalike will be recognizably "conscious," and likely as self-centered as we are. I don't mean trivial aspects of consciousness such as aware, awake, sensitive, and arousable. And I don't mean self-aware, which seems insignificant. Self-centered consciousness is, I think, going to be easy to achieve; getting it to contribute to intelligence will be harder.

It seems to me that progressive generations of workalikes will come to acquire aspects of intelligent consciousness, such as steerable attention, mental rehearsal, language production guided by syntax, abstraction, imagery, subconscious processing, "what-if" planning, strategic decision making—and especially the narratives we humans tell ourselves while we are awake or dreaming.

Though running on principles closely analogous to those used in our brains, a workalike would be carefully engineered so that it could be rebooted when difficulties arose. I can already see one way of engineering this, using those darwinian essentials and the cortical wiring patterns that lead to triangular arrays and thus to hexagonal copying competitions among variants and hybrids. To the extent that such functions can operate far faster than they do in our own millisecond-scale brains, we'll see an aspect of "superhuman" abilities emerging from the workalike. If workalikes are able to achieve new levels of organization (meta-metaphors!), it may point the way to educate humans to make the same step.

But that's the easy part—the extrapolation of existing trends in computing technology, AI, plus the neuropsychological and neurophysiological understanding of human brains. Refining wisdom out of knowledge does, of course, take a lot longer than refining knowledge out of data. And there are at least three hard parts.

> *The world of the future will be an even more*
> *demanding struggle against the limitations of our*
> *intelligence, not a comfortable hammock in*
> *which we can lie down to be waited upon by our*
> *robot slaves.*
> NORBERT WIENER, 1950

ONE HARD PART will be to make sure a superhuman intelligence fits into an ecology comprised of animal species. Such as us.

Especially us. That's because competition is most intense between closely related species—which is the reason that none of our Australopithecine and *Homo erectus* cousins are still around, the reason why only two omnivorous ape species have survived. (The other apes are vegetarians, with long guts to extract the meager calories from all that high-bulk food.) Our more immediate ancestors probably wiped out the other ape and hominid species as competitors, if climate change didn't.

"To keep every wheel and cog," said the environmentalist Aldo Leopold in 1948, "is the first precaution of intelligent tinkering." Introducing a powerful new species into the ecosystem is not a step to be taken lightly.

When automation rearrangements occur so gradually that no one starves, they are often beneficial. Everyone used to gather or hunt their own food, but agricultural technologies have gradually reduced the percentage of the population that farms to about 3 percent in the industrialized countries. And that's freed up many people to spend their time at other pursuits. The relative mix of those occupations changes over time, as in the shift from manufacturing jobs to service jobs in recent decades. A century ago, the two largest occupational groups in the developed countries were farmworkers and household servants. Now they're a small fraction of the total.

Workalikes, however, will displace even some of the more educated workers; those of poor education or below-average intelligence will have even bleaker prospects than they do now. But there could be some significant benefits to humans: imagine a superhuman teaching machine as a teacher's assistant, one that could hold actual conversations with students, never got bored with drills, always remembered to provide the necessary variety to keep the students interested, could tailor the offerings to a student's particular needs, and could routinely scan for signs of such developmental disorders as dyslexia or poor attention span.

Silicon superhumans could also apply their talents to teaching the next generation of superhumans, evolving still smarter ones just by variation and selection: after all, their star silicon pupil could be cloned. Each clone would be educated somewhat differently thereafter. With varied experiences, some might acquire desirable traits—values such as sociability or concern for human welfare. Again, we could select the "best" pupil for cloning. Since the copying includes memories to date (that's the other advantage of intelligence *in silico* besides rebooting: you can include readout capabilities for use in cloning), experience would be cumulative and truly Lamarckian: the offspring wouldn't have to repeat the parent's mistakes.

VALUES ARE THE SECOND HARD PART: agreeing on them and implementing them *in silico*.

The first-order workalikes will be just as amoral as our pets or a young child—just raw intelligence and language ability. They won't even come with the inherited qualities that make our pets safe to be around. We humans tend to be treated by our pets as either their mother (in the case of cats) or as their pack leader (in the case of dogs); they defer to us. This cognitive confusion on their part allows us to benefit from their inborn social behaviors. We'll probably want something similar in our intelligent machines, but since they'll be a lot more capable of doing mischief than our pets are, we'll probably want real safeguards—something fancier than muzzles, leashes, and fences.

How do we build in safeguards as abstract as Isaac Asimov's Laws of Robotics? My guess is that it will require a lot of star-pupil cloning, a process not unlike the domestication of the dog. This gradual evolution over many superhuman generations might partially substitute for biological inheritance at birth, perhaps minimizing any possible sociopathic tendencies in silicon superhumans and limiting their risk-taking behaviors.

If that's true, it will take many decades to get from raw intelligence (that first-order workalike) to a safe-without-constant-supervision superhuman. The early models could be smart and talkative without being cautious or wise—a very risky combination, potentially sociopathic. They would have the top-end abilities without those abilities' well-tested evolutionary predecessors as the underpinning.

> *Declare the past, diagnose the present, foretell
> the future.*
>
> Hippocrates of Cos (460–377 B.C.),
> advice to physicians

THE THIRD HARD PART is moderating the reactions of humanity to the perceived challenge. Just as an overenthusiastic reaction by your immune system to an antigen can cripple you via allergies and autoimmune diseases (and perhaps kill you by anaphylactic shock), so human reactions to silicon superhumans could create enormous strains in our present civilization. A serious reaction, once workalikes were already playing a significant role in the economy, could disrupt the system that allows the farmers to feed the other 97 percent of us. Remember that famines kill because the distribution system fails, not because there isn't enough food grown somewhere in the world.

But the Luddites and *sabots* of the twenty-first century will be aided by some very basic features of human ethology— ones which played little role in nineteenth-century Europe. Groups try to distinguish themselves from others. Despite the benefits of a common language, most tribes in history have exaggerated linguistic differences with their neighbors, so as to tell friend from foe. You can be sure that the Turing Test will be in regular use, with people trying to determine whether a real human is at the other end of the phone line. Machines could be required to speak in a characteristic voice to dampen this anxiety, but that won't be enough to prevent "us and them" tensions.

Workalikes and superhumans could also be restricted to certain occupations. Their entry into other areas could be subject to an evaluation process that carefully tested a new model against a sample of real human society. When the potential for serious side effects is so great, and the rate of introduction is potentially rapid, we would be well advised to adopt procedures similar to how the FDA tests new drugs and medical instruments for efficacy, safety, and side effects. This would not slow the development of the technology so much as it would slow its widespread use, and allow for a retreat before too great a dependency developed.

Workalikes might be restricted to a limited sphere of interactions; they might require stringent licensing to use the Internet or telephone networks. There might be a one-day-delay rule for distributing output from superhumans that only had a beginner's license, to address some of the "program trading" hazards. For some fledgling workalikes, we might want the computer equivalent of a biohazard containment for lethal viruses.

> *The search for truth is predatory. It is a literal hunt, a conquest. There is that exemplary instant in Book IV of* The Republic, *when Socrates and his companions in discourse corner an abstract truth. They halloo, like hunters who have unearthed and run down their quarry. . . . [Even if enjoined from the scientific quest,] somewhere, at some moment, a man alone, a group of men addicted to the drug of absolute thought, will be seeking to create organic tissue, to determine the nature of heredity, to produce the cloud-chamber trail of quarks. Not for renown, not for the benefit of the human species, not in the name of social justice or profit, but because of a drive stronger than love, stronger than even hatred,* which is to be interested in something. *For its own enigmatic sake. Because it is there.*
> GEORGE STEINER, 1978

THESE CONSIDERATIONS DO START TO RAISE THE QUESTION: "Just what *is* the proper business of this society of ours?" Making humans "all they can be" by removing shackles and optimizing upbringing? Or making computers better than humans? Maybe we can do both (as in those teacher's assistants), but during our headlong rush to produce superhumans—a major form of tinkering—we need to protect humanity.

The ways in which we could introduce caution, however, are constrained by the various drives that are leading us to this intelligence transition:

- Curiosity is my own primary motivation—how does intelligence come about?—and surely that of many computer scientists. But even if because-it-is-there curiosity were somehow hobbled (as various religions have attempted), other drives lead us in the same direction.

- The technology version of the Red Queen Effect. If we don't improve the technology, someone else will. Historically, losing technological races has often meant being taken over (or eliminated) by your competitor—and on the scale of nations, not just companies. Given those doubling-every-eighteen-months growth curves in speed and megabytes over the last several decades in digital computers, the rest of the world probably wouldn't slow down even if the majority decided to do so. As the phrase goes in the biotech business, "They'll just do it offshore."

- Serious environmental threats to civilization demand the development of huge computing resources: our climate can "shift gears" in only a few years when a rearrangement of ocean currents occurs. Such a sudden flip now (and global warming appears to make a flip more likely, not less) would set off World War III, as everyone (not just the Europeans) struggled for *Lebensraum*. It is urgent, for our own survival, that we learn how to postpone those climatic gearshifts. The big computers needed for global climatic modeling are very similar to what one would need for simulating brain processes.

I don't see realistic ways of buying time to make this superhuman transition at a more deliberate pace. And so the problems of superintelligent machines will simply need to be faced head-on in the next several decades, not somehow postponed by slowing technological progress.

Our civilization will, of course, be "playing God" in an ultimate sense of the phrase: evolving a greater intelligence than currently exists on earth. It behooves us to be a considerate creator, wise to the world and its fragile nature, sensitive to the need for stable footings that will prevent backsliding—and keep that house of cards we call civilization from collapsing.

*Only two centuries ago, we could explain
everything about everything, out of pure reason,
and now most of that elaborate and harmonious
structure has come apart before our eyes. We are
dumb. . . . We have discovered how to ask
important questions, and now we really do need,
as an urgent matter, some answers. We now know
that we cannot do this any longer by searching
our minds, for there is not enough there to
search, nor can we find the truth by guessing at it
or by making up stories for ourselves. We cannot
stop where we are, stuck with today's level of
understanding, nor can we go back. I do not see
that we have any real choice in this, for I can see
only the one way ahead. We need science, more
and better science, not for its technology, not for
leisure, not even for health and longevity, but for
the hope of wisdom which our kind of culture
must acquire for its survival.*

Lewis Thomas, 1979

RECOMMENDED READING

DEREK BICKERTON, *Language and Species* (University of Chicago Press, 1990).

DEREK BICKERTON, *Language and Human Behavior* (University of Washington Press, 1995).

WILLIAM H. CALVIN, *The Ascent of Mind: Ice Age Climates and the Evolution of Intelligence* (Bantam, 1990). World Wide Web links to most of the author's books can be found at **http://weber.u. washington.edu/~wcalvin/.**

WILLIAM H. CALVIN, *The Cerebral Code* (MIT Press, 1996).

WILLIAM H. CALVIN and GEORGE A. OJEMANN, *Conversations with Neil's Brain: The Neural Nature of Thought and Language* (Addison-Wesley, 1994).

PAUL M. CHURCHLAND, *The Engine of Reason, the Seat of the Soul* (MIT Press, 1995).

DANIEL C. DENNETT, *Consciousness Explained* (Little, Brown, 1991).

DANIEL C. DENNETT, *Darwin's Dangerous Idea* (Simon & Schuster, 1995).

MERLIN DONALD, *Origins of the Modern Mind* (Harvard University Press, 1991).

OWEN FLANAGAN, *Consciousness Reconsidered* (MIT Press, 1992).

WALTER J. FREEMAN, *Societies of Brains* (Erlbaum, 1995).

JAMES L. GOULD and CAROL GRANT GOULD, *The Animal Mind* (Scientific American Library, 1994).

J. ALLAN HOBSON, *The Chemistry of Conscious States: How the Brain Changes Its Mind* (Little, Brown, 1994).

NICHOLAS K. HUMPHREY, *Consciousness Regained* (Oxford University Press, 1984).

RAY JACKENDOFF, *Patterns in the Mind: Language and Human Nature* (Basic Books, 1994).

165

MARVIN MINSKY, *The Society of Mind* (Simon & Schuster, 1986).

STEVEN PINKER, *The Language Instinct* (Morrow, 1994).

ROBERT J. RICHARDS, *Darwin and the Emergence of Evolutionary Theories of Mind and Behavior* (University of Chicago Press, 1987).

SUE SAVAGE-RUMBAUGH and ROGER LEWIN, *Kanzi: The Ape at the Brink of the Human Mind* (Wiley, 1994).

Scientific American special issues on the brain (September 1979 and September 1992), "Life in the Universe" (October 1994).

REFERENCE BOOKS
••••••••••••

PATRICIA S. CHURCHLAND and TERRANCE J. SEJNOWSKI, *The Computational Brain* (MIT Press, 1992).

PIETRO CORSI, editor, *The Enchanted Loom: Chapters in the History of Neuroscience* (Oxford University Press, 1991).

STANLEY FINGER, *Origins of Neuroscience: A History of Explorations into Brain Function* (Oxford University Press, 1994).

RICHARD GREGORY, editor, *The Oxford Companion to the Mind* (Oxford University Press, 1987).

EUAN M. MACPHAIL, *The Neuroscience of Animal Intelligence* (Columbia University Press, 1993). Intelligence, in the sense used in the present book, is only briefly addressed in the closing pages; it's mostly about associative learning in simple systems, memory research, and other foundations for intelligence.

NOTES

···

I. WHAT TO DO NEXT
···········

1   Sören Kierkegaard, *Collected Works* (1843/1901).

1   Sue Savage-Rumbaugh and Roger Lewin, *Kanzi: The Ape at the Brink of the Human Mind* (Wiley, 1994), p. 255.

2   Antonio Damasio, Daniel Tranel, "Nouns and verbs are retrieved with differently distributed neural systems," *Proceedings of the National Academy of Sciences (U.S.A.)* 90:4757–4760 (1993).

2   Intelligence researchers avoid consciousness: of all the authors of the *Handbook of Human Intelligence* (R. J. Sternberg, editor; Cambridge University Press, 1982), only one even mentions consciousness in passing.

3   La Mettrie and Descartes history from Claudio Pogliano, "Between form and function: a new science of man," in *The Enchanted Loom: Chapters in the History of Neuroscience*, edited by Pietro Corsi (Oxford University Press, 1991), pp. 144–157, at p. 145.

5   William James's 1870s ideas, cited in Robert J. Richards, *Darwin and the Emergence of Evolutionary Theories of Mind and Behavior* (University of Chicago Press, 1987), pp. 433ff.

6   Pygmy chimpanzees, or bonobos, can be seen in some numbers at the zoos of San Diego, Cincinnati, Washington, D.C., Frankfurt, Hanover, and Antwerp. In the wild, they live only in one small region of swampy forest, on the equator at 21–22° E longitude, in the Congo River basin of Zaire. They have no protected park land and are an endangered species, despite being behaviorally our closest primate cousins. See chapter 4 of Savage-Rumbaugh and Lewin (1994) and Frans B. M. de Waal, "Bonobo sex and society," *Scientific American*

167

272(4):82–88 (March 1995). See the web page **http://weber.u.washington.edu/~wcalvin/bonobo.html**

2. EVOLVING A GOOD GUESS
••••••••••••

9   James L. Gould and Carol Grant Gould, *The Animal Mind* (Scientific American Library, 1994), pp. 68–70.

10   T. Edward Reed, Arthur R. Jensen, "Conduction velocity in a brain nerve pathway of normal adults correlates with intelligence level," *Intelligence* 16:14 (1992).

10   A good summary of IQ and its racial differences, in a statement signed by dozens of the leading researchers, may be found (of all places) in the *Wall Street Journal*, p. A18 (13 December 1994). See Earl Hunt's "The role of intelligence in modern society," *American Scientist* 83:356–368 (July–August 1995).

12   Barbara L. Finlay and Richard B. Darlington argue, in "Linked regularities in the development and evolution of mammalian brains," *Science* 268:1578–1584 (16 June 1995), that if a human ancestor were selected for *any non-olfactory capacity* requiring more brain space, the brain space for all others would be increased in parallel.

12   A. J. Rockel, R. W. Hiorns, T. P. S. Powell, "The basic uniformity in structure of the neocortex," *Brain* 103:221–244 (1980).

13   Bertrand Russell, *Philosophy* (Norton, 1927).

13   See the last chapter of Jean Piaget, *The Origins of Intelligence in Children* (translation of *La naissance de l'intelligence chez l'enfant*, 1923).

14   H. B. Barlow, in *Oxford Companion to the Mind* (1987). See also Haneef A. Fatmi and R. W. Young, "A definition of intelligence," *Nature* 228:97 (1970): "Intelligence is that faculty of mind by which order is perceived in a situation previously considered disordered." Note how close this comes to the mathematician's definition of *chaos* (finding order among apparent randomness).

14   Infant soothing: Sandra E. Trehub, University of Toronto, personal communication (1995).

14   Donald N. Michael, "Forecasting and planning in an incoherent context," *Technological Forecasting and Social Change* 36:79–87 (1989).

15   Frans de Waal, *Peacemaking Among Primates* (Harvard University Press, 1989).

15   Gould and Gould (1994), p. 149.

15   " . . . slip the bounds of instinct . . . " is from Gould and Gould (1994), p. 70.

16   J. P. Guilford, "Traits of creativity," in *Creativity and Its Cultivation*, edited by H. H. Anderson (Harper, 1959), pp. 142–161.

17   Chimpanzee understanding of spoken requests vs. symbolic ones: the 1993 videos of Sue Savage-Rumbaugh's research address these issues. The footage appears in the commonly available BBC and NOVA edits of the original NHK production, usually entitled *Kanzi*. The researchers also have a privately circulated videotape of techniques and negative results.

17   STANLEY COREN, *The Intelligence of Dogs: Canine Consciousness and Capabilities* (Free Press, 1994), pp. 114–115.

18   RICHARD BYRNE, ANDREW WHITEN, editors, *Machiavellian Intelligence: Social Expertise and the Evolution of Intellect in Monkeys, Apes, and Humans* (Oxford University Press, 1988).

19   KENNETH J. W. CRAIK, *The Nature of Explanation* (Cambridge University Press, 1943).

20   Birds and hawks: See IRENÄUS EIBL-EIBESFELDT, *Ethology* (Holt, Rinehart, & Winston, 1975), pp. 87–88.

20   Random elements in music: BRIAN ENO, personal communication (1995). Disordered sensations not signaling harm but mistakenly perceived as painful: WILLIAM H. CALVIN, *The Throwing Madonna* (McGraw-Hill, 1983). Perhaps if multiple sclerosis and phantom-limb patients became accustomed to heavy metal music, they could learn to love their disordered sensations, too! Or at least treat them as not really threatening.

21   LOREN EISELEY, *The Star Thrower* (Times Books, 1978).

22   Neoteny is discussed by STEPHEN JAY GOULD, *Ontogeny and Phylogeny* (Harvard University Press, 1977), pp. 177ff; BARRY BOGIN, *Patterns of Human Growth* (Cambridge University Press, 1988), p. 71; ASHLEY MONTAGU, *Growing Young* (McGraw-Hill, 1981); and F. HARVEY POUGH, JOHN B. HEISER, and WILLIAM N. MCFARLAND, *Vertebrate Life*, 3rd edition (Macmillan, 1989), p. 68. Such shifts in domestication are noted by COREN (1994), pp. 37–41.

22   For the story of the Japanese monkeys, see chapter 3 in my book of essays, *The Throwing Madonna* (McGraw-Hill, 1983).

23   PATRICIA S. GOLDMAN-RAKIC, "Working memory and the mind," *Scientific American* 267(3):73–79 (September 1992).

23   The bee navigation story is in GOULD and GOULD (1994).

23   JACOB BRONOWSKI, *The Origins of Knowledge and Imagination* (Yale University Press, 1978, transcribed from 1967 lectures), p. 33.

24   "Hunter plotting various approaches. . . . " Much of hunting in carnivores is determined by some simple innate behaviors, such as "encircle the prey" (dogs that herd animals are following this same innate tendency). The big cats clearly do not understand certain principles such as "stay downwind," and may spook their prey in a way that human hunters can avoid. See COREN (1994).

24   "A futurist spinning three scenarios," see PETER SCHWARTZ, *The Art of the Long View* (Doubleday, 1991), or JOEL GARREAU's magazine article on the Global Business Network in *WIRED* 2.11 (November 1994).

25   Back in slide-rule days, students were actually taught to guess the answer before moving their slipstick. That's because slide rules don't give you the order of magnitude: 2.044 at the index mark still needs to be interpreted as .2, 2, 20, 204, and so on. So the student

would look through the equation and guess whether the answer ought to be dozens or hundreds or thousands. The advent of hand calculators has eliminated this as a necessary step, but it remains one of the best ways of catching errors. A modern application is mentally estimating prices from exchange rates while traveling abroad.
25 Gould and Gould (1994), p. 163.

3. THE JANITOR'S DREAM
••••••••••
27 Daniel C. Dennett, *Consciousness Explained* (Little, Brown, 1991), pp. 21–22.
28 Owen Flanagan, *Consciousness Reconsidered* (MIT Press, 1992). The new mysterians believe that natural phenomena in the brain can account for consciousness, but that the subject is terminally mysterious because it is cognitively closed to us; some greater intelligence might be able to understand it all, but not us mere mortals. Placing consciousness, as some do, in some quantum mechanical field that we experience as free will and "mind" is merely replacing one mystery with another; there are no parts and pieces of this explanation that we can recombine to predict the many phenomena (including characteristic mistakes) of conscious experience.
29 Notable exception: John C. Eccles, *How the Self Controls Its Brain* (Springer-Verlag, 1994).
29 William H. Calvin, *The Cerebral Symphony: Seashore Reflections on the Structure of Consciousness* (Bantam, 1989).
30 Paul M. Churchland, *The Engine of Reason, the Seat of the Soul* (MIT Press, 1995).
31 Francis Crick and Christof Koch, "The problem of consciousness," *Scientific American* 267(3):152–159 (September 1992).
31 Francis Crick, *The Astonishing Hypothesis* (Simon & Schuster, 1994).
33 E. H. Gombrich, *Art and Illusion: A Study in the Psychology of Pictorial Representation* (Princeton University Press, 1960), p. 172.
33 A. N. Meltzoff, M. K. Moore, "Imitation of facial and manual gestures by human neonates," *Science* 198:75–78 (1977). There are, of course, arguments that some of what seems to be imitation is really just the stimulus *releasing* an inborn movement pattern, for example, R. W. Byrne, "The evolution of intelligence," in *Behaviour and Evolution*, edited by P. J. B. Slater and T. R. Halliday (Cambridge University Press, 1994), pp. 223–265.
34 Elisabetta Visalberghi, M. C. Riviello, A. Blasetti, "Mirror responses in tufted capuchin monkeys (*Cebus apella*)," *Monitore Zoologico Italiano* 22:487–556 (1988).
35 Douglas R. Hofstadter, *Metamagical Themas* (Basic Books, 1985), p. 787.
36 Stratified stability, see Jacob Bronowski, *The Origins of Knowledge*

and Imagination (Yale University Press, 1978, transcribed from 1967 lectures), p. 33.

40 William James, *Talks to Teachers on Psychology and to Students on Some of Life's Ideals* (H. Holt, 1899), p. 159.

41 Gilbert Ryle, *The Concept of Mind* (Hutchinson, 1949).

43 Preparation for movement as the goal of sensation has long been a theme of neurophysiological thought: see Marc Jennerod, *The Brain Machine: The Development of Neurophysiological Thought* (Harvard University Press, 1985; translation from *Le cerveau-machine: physiologie de la volonté*, 1983).

45 Derek Bickerton, *Language and Species* (University of Chicago Press, 1990), p. 86.

4. EVOLVING INTELLIGENT ANIMALS
••••••••••••

47 Sue Savage-Rumbaugh and Roger Lewin, *Kanzi: The Ape at the Brink of the Human Mind* (Wiley, 1994), p. 260.

47 Proximate and ultimate causation, see Ernst Mayr, *The Growth of Biological Thought* (Harvard University Press, 1982).

48 Donald R. Griffin, *Animal Thinking* (Harvard University Press, 1984).

50 Nicholas Humphrey's book *The Inner Eye* (Faber and Faber, 1986) is a good exposition on the role of social life in shaping up intelligence.

50 Birute M. F. Galdikas, *Reflections of Eden: My Years with the Orangutans of Borneo* (Little, Brown, 1995).

51 Sexual selection for language abilities, see William H. Calvin, "The unitary hypothesis: a common neural circuitry for novel manipulations, language, plan-ahead, and throwing?" in *Tools, Language, and Cognition in Human Evolution*, edited by Kathleen R. Gibson and Tim Ingold (Cambridge University Press, 1993), pp. 230–250. On the web at **http://weber.u.washington.edu/~wcalvin/unitary.html**

51 Nicholas Humphrey, *Consciousness Regained* (Oxford University Press, 1984), chapter 2.

52 William H. Calvin, *The Ascent of Mind: Ice Age Climates and the Evolution of Intelligence* (Bantam, 1990), chapter 5.

53 John Eliot Allen and Marjorie Burns, *Cataclysms on the Columbia* (Portland: Timber Press, 1986).

55 Michael H. Field, Brian Huntley, Helmut Müller, "Eemian climate fluctuations observed in a European pollen record," *Nature* 371:779–783 (27 October 1994).

55 Wallace S. Broecker, "Massive iceberg discharges as triggers for global climate change," *Nature* 372:421–424 (1 December 1994), and his "Chaotic climate," *Scientific American* 273(5):62–69 (November 1995).

55 W. Dansgaard, S. J. Johnsen, H. B. Clausen, D. Dahl-Jensen, N. S.

GUNDESTRUP, C. U. HAMMER, C. S. HVIDBERG, J. P. STEFFENSEN, A. E. SVEIN-BJORNSDOTTIR, J. JOUZEL, G. BOND, "Evidence for general instability of past climate from a 250-kyr ice-core record," *Nature* 364:218–221 (15 July 1993).

55 W. DANSGAARD, W. J. C. WHITE, S. J. JOHNSEN, "The abrupt termination of the Younger Dryas climate event," *Nature* 339:532–535 (15 July 1989).

55 RICHARD J. BEHL, JAMES P. KENNETT, "Brief interstadial events in the Santa Barbara basin, NE Pacific, during the past 60 kyr," *Nature* 379:243–246 (18 January 1996).

56 The beginning of the ice age at 2.51 million years ago is dated by N. J. SHACKLETON, J. BACKMAN, H. ZIMMERMAN, D. V. KENT, M. A. HALL, D. G. ROBERTS, D. SCHNITKER, J. G. BALDAUF, A. DESPRAIRIES, R. HOMRIGHAUSEN, P. HUDDLESTUN, J. B. KEENE, A. J. KALTENBACK, K. A. O. KRUMSIEK, A. C. MORTON, J. W. MURRAY, and J. WESTBERG-SMITH, "Oxygen isotope calibration of the onset of ice-rafting and history of glaciation in the North Atlantic region," *Nature* 307:620–623 (1984).

56 Ice-age astronomical rhythms from changes in high-latitude sunlight, see JOHN IMBRIE and KATHERINE P. IMBRIE, *Ice Ages* (Harvard University Press, 1986).

59 STEVEN PINKER, *The Language Instinct* (Morrow, 1994), p. 363.

61 GORDON H. BOWER, DANIEL G. MORROW, "Mental models in narrative comprehension," *Science* 247:44–48 (1990).

61 SVEN BIRKERTS, *The Gutenberg Elegies: The Fate of Reading in an Electronic Age* (Faber and Faber, 1994), p. 84.

5. SYNTAX AS A FOUNDATION OF INTELLIGENCE
• • • • • • • • • • • •

63 DEREK BICKERTON, *Language and Species* (University of Chicago Press, 1990), p. 157.

64 OLIVER SACKS, *Seeing Voices* (University of California Press, 1989), pp. 40–44.

65 PATRICIA K. KUHL, KAREN A. WILLIAMS, FRANCISCO LACERDA, KENNETH N. STEVENS, BJORN LINDBLOM, "Linguistic experience alters phonetic perception in infants by 6 months of age," *Science* 255:606–608 (31 January 1992).

65 Vervet vocalizations, see ROBERT M. SEYFARTH, "Vocal communication and its relation to language," in *Primate Societies*, edited by Barbara M. Smuts et al. (University of Chicago Press, 1986), pp. 440–451.

66 Bee dance as language: compare JAMES L. GOULD and CAROL GRANT GOULD, *The Animal Mind* (Scientific American Library, 1994), with ADRIAN M. WENNER, D. MEADE, and L. J. FRIESEN, "Recruitment, search behavior, and flight ranges of honey bees," *American Zoologist* 31(6):768–782 (1991).

67 BICKERTON (1990), excerpt at pp. 15–16.

67 STANLEY COREN, *The Intelligence of Dogs: Canine Consciousness and Capabilities* (Free Press, 1994), pp. 114–115.

68   E. Sue Savage-Rumbaugh, Jeannine Murphy, Rose A. Sevcik, Karen E. Brakke, Shelley L. Williams, and Duane Rumbaugh, *Language Comprehension in Ape and Child* (University of Chicago Press, 1993). Monographs of the Society for Research on Child Development 58(3).

69   Sue Savage-Rumbaugh and Roger Lewin, *Kanzi: The Ape at the Brink of the Human Mind* (Wiley, 1994), p. 60.

69   Ray Jackendoff, *Patterns in the Mind: Language and Human Nature* (Basic Books, 1994), p. 138.

69   "Bonobos inventing rules . . . ," see Savage-Rumbaugh and Lewin (1994), p. 162.

70   Jackendoff (1994), p. 14.

72   Duane M. Rumbaugh, personal communication (1995).

73   Immigrants' difficulties were studied by Jacqueline S. Johnson and Elissa L. Newport, "Critical period effects in second language learning: the influence of maturational state on the acquisition of English as a second language," *Cognitive Psychology* 21:60–99 (1989).

74   Bickerton (1990), pp. 55–56.

76   Bickerton (1990), pp. 60–61.

77   Bickerton (1990), p. 66.

77   Animal comprehension issue, see Savage-Rumbaugh et al. (1993).

78   Savage-Rumbaugh and Lewin (1994), p. 174.

88   Kathryn Morton, "The story-telling animal," *New York Times Book Review*, pp. 1–2 (23 December 1984).

89   Savage-Rumbaugh and Lewin (1994), p. 264.

89   Bickerton (1990), p. 257.

6. EVOLUTION ON-THE-FLY
••••••••••••

91   John Stuart Mill, *Auguste Comte and Positivism* (1865).

92   Chunking: Herbert A. Simon, *Models of Thought* (Yale University Press, 1979), p. 41.

93   George A. Miller, "The magical number seven, plus or minus two: some limits on our capacity for processing information," *Psychological Reviews* 63:81–97 (1956).

93   Chunking and short-term memory span, see Philip Lieberman, *Uniquely Human: The Evolution of Speech, Thought, and Selfless Behavior* (Harvard University Press, 1991), p. 82.

95   Charles Darwin, *The Origin of Species* (John Murray, 1859), p. 137.

97   Speaking of spitting, it, too, is ballistic. Exactly the same slow feedback problems occur with speech, on the timescale of many short words: you can't modify the end of the word if your tongue trips on the first syllable. Words, too, can be ballistic, when spit out rather than slowly rolled out. The feedback loop from the lip proprioceptors is about 70 msec.

97   The launch window is essentially the permissible range of error for the time of the peak angular velocity (after that, the projectile tends to fly loose of the hand's grip).

97 "Average out" in the sense of an ensemble average rather than the usual time average. "Not locked together" means that as long as each neuron's noise is statistically independent of the noise of the others, it is an independent random source. We're edging around what is known as the Law of Large Numbers; see, for example, WILLIAM H. CALVIN, "A stone's throw and its launch window: timing precision and its implications for language and hominid brains," *Journal of Theoretical Biology* 104:121–135 (1983). My subsequent book *The Ascent of Mind* (1990) has the more modern set of arguments for the hypothesis in the later chapters.

98 CHARLES DARWIN, *The Expression of the Emotions in Man and Animals* (John Murray, 1872). Quoted at p. 177 in *The Darwin Reader*, edited by MARK RIDLEY (Norton, 1987).

99 "Prefrontal" is a terrible name. What it means, roughly, is the part of the frontal lobe in front of the premotor cortex, that is, the prepremotor frontal lobe.

100 PAUL J. ESLINGER, ANTONIO R. DAMASIO, "Severe disturbances of higher cognition after bilateral frontal lobe ablation: patient E.V.R.," *Neurology* 35:1731–1741 (1985). For a fuller discussion, see DAMASIO's book *Descartes' Error* (Putnam's, 1995).

100 DOREEN KIMURA, "Sex differences in the brain," *Scientific American* 267(3):118–125 (September 1992).

100 GEORGE A. OJEMANN, "Electrical stimulation and the neurobiology of language," *Behavioral and Brain Science* 6:221–226 (1983). See also WILLIAM H. CALVIN and GEORGE A. OJEMANN, *Conversations with Neil's Brain: The Neural Nature of Thought and Language* (Addison-Wesley, 1994).

102 ROBERT FROST, in *Selected Prose of Robert Frost,* edited by H. COX and E. C. LATHEM (Collier, 1986), pp. 33–46.

102 The excerpt is from an English translation of UMBERTO ECO's back-page column, "La bustina di Minerva," in the Italian newsweekly *Espresso* (September 30, 1994).

103 KENNETH J. W. CRAIK, *The Nature of Explanation* (Cambridge University Press, 1943), p. 61.

104 The Darwin Machine terminology actually preceded the list of six essentials: WILLIAM H. CALVIN, "The brain as a Darwin Machine," *Nature* 330:33–34 (5 November 1987).

104 My six essentials really aren't much different than the three which ALFRED RUSSEL WALLACE listed in 1875 (" . . . the known laws of variation, multiplication, and heredity . . . have probably sufficed . . . "); it's just that I make explicit the pattern, the work space competition, and the environmental biases. See WALLACE's "The limits of natural selection as applied to man," chapter 10 of *Contributions to the Theory of Natural Selection* (Macmillan, 1875). See also the use of darwinian principles in computation: "genetic algorithms" can be found in JOHN H. HOLLAND, *Adaptation in Natural and Artificial Systems* (MIT Press, 1992).

107 Musical scale analogy: since neurons aren't lined up in a row like piano keys, the musical scale analogy isn't quite right. A reader-board (or computer display pixel about 14 × 14) is probably closer, the "melody" being envisaged as an animated abstract cartoon that plays on the little screen.

108 DONALD O. HEBB, *The Organization of Behavior* (Wiley, 1949). See PETER M. MILNER, "The mind and Donald O. Hebb," *Scientific American* 268(1):124–129 (January 1993).

108 LEWIS THOMAS, *The Medusa and the Snail* (Viking, 1979), p. 154.

109 While *long-term* potentiation (LTP) was named for a version that lasted many days in the hippocampus, the process in the neocortex seems to last only for about five minutes (see IRIKI et al. [1991], below), placing LTP squarely in the camp of a *short-term* memory process. It may, of course, have lingering components that provide the scaffolding for a more permanent change in synaptic strengths via anatomical changes in the number and contact area of boutons.

109 ISRAEL ROSENFIELD, *The Strange, Familiar, and Forgotten: An Anatomy of Consciousness* (Knopf, 1992), p. 87.

110 The most impressive spatiotemporal patterns in cerebral cortex are those demonstrated by E. VAADIA, I. HAALMAN, M. ABELES, H. BERGMAN, Y. PRUT, H. SLOVIN, and A. AERTSEN, "Dynamics of neuronal interactions in monkey cortex in relation to behaviourial events," *Nature* 373:515–518 (9 February 1995). For an exposition on mass action in nervous systems and the emergence of spatiotemporal patterning, see WALTER J. FREEMAN, *Societies of Brains* (Erlbaum, 1995).

110 J. ALLAN HOBSON, *The Chemistry of Conscious States: How the Brain Changes Its Mind* (Little, Brown, 1994).

112 GORDON H. BOWER, DANIEL G. MORROW, "Mental models in narrative comprehension," *Science* 247:44–48 (1990).

112 DEREK BICKERTON, *Language and Species* (University of Chicago, 1990), p. 249.

7. SHAPING UP AN INTELLIGENT ACT FROM HUMBLE ORIGINS
••••••••••••

113 IMMANUEL KANT, *Kritik der reinen Vernunft* (1787).

113 LEWIS CARROLL, *Alice's Adventures in Wonderland* (Macmillan, 1865).

114 If you are sufficiently comfortable with neurophysiology and cerebral circuitry, you can go on to read my academic book, *The Cerebral Code*, for more. The background is in WILLIAM H. CALVIN, "Islands in the mind: dynamic subdivisions of association cortex and the emergence of a Darwin Machine," *Seminars in the Neurosciences* 3(5):423–433 (1991). WILLIAM H. CALVIN, "The emergence of intelligence," *Scientific American* 271(4):100–107 (October 1994; also appears in the Scientific American book *Life in the Universe*, 1995— N.B., the hexagons figure is an editorial error; simply ignore it or see the web page **http://weber.u.washington.edu/~wcalvin/sciamer.html** for the unaltered version).

115 This account of cortical neuroanatomy is necessarily brief; a somewhat more extensive account of cells, circuits, neurotransmitters, and computation is in chapter 6 of WILLIAM H. CALVIN and GEORGE A. OJE-MANN, *Conversations with Neil's Brain: The Neural Nature of Thought and Language* (Addison-Wesley, 1994).

117 Convergence zones, see ANTONIO R. DAMASIO, "Time-locked multi-regional retroactivation: a systems-level proposal for the neural substrates of recall and recognition," *Cognition* 33:25–62 (1989).

119 This is an abbreviated version of the cortical columns story. See WILLIAM H. CALVIN, "Cortical columns, modules, and Hebbian cell assemblies," in *Handbook of Brain Theory and Neural Networks*, edited by M. A. ARBIB (MIT Press, 1995), pp. 269–272.

121 For a pattern to "mean the same thing . . .," even though shifted, simply says that it is still capable of copying and engaging in the other processes that eventually lead to the characteristic output pattern, for example, pronouncing a noun.

124 NMDA is *N*-methyl-D-aspartate; it's even better than glutamate at opening these ion channels, even though plain old glutamate is what is used by the synaptic neurotransmission. NMDA was named back in the days when receptor types were thought to be few in number, and they were named for their currently best agonist. Now there are so many that they're using serial numbers.

124 ATSUSHI IRIKI, CONSTANTINE PAVLIDES, ASAF KELLER, HIROSHI ASANUMA, "Long-term potentiation of thalamic input to the motor cortex induced by coactivation of thalamocortical and corticocortical afferents," *Journal of Neurophysiology* 65:1435–1441 (1991).

124 Memory classifications, and their thoroughly confusing terminology, are explained in chapter 7 of CALVIN and OJEMANN (1994).

125 JENNIFER S. LUND, TAKASHI YOSHIOKA, JONATHAN B. LEVITT, "Comparison of intrinsic connectivity in different areas of macaque monkey cerebral cortex," *Cerebral Cortex* 3:148–162 (March/April 1993).

127 "Input from neighbors. . . ." Actually, not from immediate neighbors but from voices about sixteen singers away, on all sides. It would be interesting to study a large chorus with appropriately wired intercoms, For example, your earphone would receive six inputs, mixed from the microphones of just those.

127 DAVID SOMERS, NANCY KOPELL, "Rapid synchronization through fast threshold modulation," *Biological Cybernetics* 68:393–407 (1993). see also J. T. ENRIGHT, "Temporal precision in circadian systems: a reliable neuronal clock from unreliable components?" *Science* 209:1542–1544 (1980).

130 BARBARA A. McGUIRE, CHARLES D. GILBERT, PATRICIA K. RIVLIN, TORSTEN N. WIESEL, "Targets of horizontal connections in macaque primary visual cortex," *Journal of Comparative Neurology* 305:370–392 (1991).

Also CHARLES D. GILBERT, "Circuitry, architecture, and functional dynamics of visual cortex," *Cerebral Cortex* 3:373–386 (1993).

130 WILLIAM H. CALVIN, "Error-correcting codes: coherent hexagonal copying from fuzzy neuroanatomy," *World Congress on Neural Networks* 1:101–104 (1993).

133 Making a hexagonal unit pattern from all the triangular arrays: this is true only if the component triangular arrays are parallel to one another. The ones representing colors are, fortunately, anchored in the color blobs and cannot adopt arbitrary orientations.

135 EUGEN HERRIGEL, *Zen in the Art of Archery* (Pantheon, 1953), pp. 57–58.

143 MELVIN KONNER in *On Doctoring: Stories, Poems, Essays*, edited by RICHARD REYNOLDS and JOHN STONE (Simon & Schuster, 1991).

8. PROSPECTS FOR A SUPERHUMAN INTELLIGENCE
••••••••••••

145 CHARLES E. RAVEN, *The Creator Spirit* (Harvard University Press, 1928).

147 SAMUEL TAYLOR COLERIDGE, *Biographia Literaria* (1817), chapter 14.

148 GEORGE STEINER, "Has truth a future?" Bronowski Memorial Lecture (1978), reprinted in *From Creation to Chaos*, edited by BERNARD DIXON (Basil Blackwell Ltd., 1989).

148 ROGER PENROSE, *Shadows of the Mind: A Search for the Missing Science of Consciousness* (Oxford University Press, 1994), last page. See David L. Wilson's book review in *American Scientist* (May–June 1995), pp. 269–270. For further comments by scientists and philosophers, see chapter 14 in JOHN BROCKMAN, editor, *The Third Culture* (Simon & Schuster, 1995).

149 Picking up on the notions of synchronization for binding the dispersed aspects of the analysis on an object in the brain, some have invoked quantum fields as an explanation for binding. I am led to wonder if this is not a solution in search of a problem. If the consciousness physicists were serious about this proposal, they would examine alternative ways of achieving synchrony—which are legion—and explain why their explanation was preferable to simpler explanations.

149 Discussions of unitary processes can be found in WILLIAM H. CALVIN and KATHERINE GRAUBARD, "Styles of neuronal computation." Chapter 29 in: *The Neurosciences, Fourth Study Program,* edited by F. O. SCHMITT and F. G. WORDEN (MIT Press, 1979), pp. 513–524.

149 CHRISTOPHER LEHMANN-HAUPT, "Can quantum mechanics explain consciousness?" *New York Times*, p. B2 (31 October 1994).

150 I coined "Darwin Machine" as a general mechanistic metaphor for darwinian processes that shape up complexity (*Nature*, 5 November 1987), and indeed HENRY PLOTKIN uses it in that sense in his book on evolutionary epistemology, *Darwin Machines* (Harvard University Press, 1994). My proposals for cloning competitions in neocortex are just a particular instance of a Darwin Machine.

152 William H. Calvin (1991), "The antecedents of consciousness: evolving the 'intelligent' ability to simulate situations and contemplate the consequences of novel courses of action," in *Bioastronomy: The Exploration Broadens*, edited by Jean Heidmann and Michael J. Klein (Springer-Verlag's Lecture Notes in Physics series), pp. 311–319.

152 Emphasis on up-from-movement: see Marc Jennerod, *The Brain Machine: The Development of Neurophysiological Thought* (Harvard University Press, 1985; translation from *Le cerveau-machine: physiologie de la volonté*, 1983), and, for other brain/body interrelations, Damasio (1994).

155 For some examples of what I mean by dangerous innovation, see some of the discussions of manic-depressive illness, such as in Kay Redfield Jamison, *Touched with Fire: Manic-Depressive Illness and the Artistic Temperament* (Free Press, 1993), and her autobiography, *An Unquiet Mind: A Memoir of Moods and Madness* (Knopf, 1995).

155 Stephen Jay Gould, *The Flamingo's Smile* (Norton, 1985), p. 431.

156 Thomas F. Mandel, see links from web page **http://weber.u.washington.edu/~wcalvin/mandel.html**.

156 Marvin Minsky, "Will robots inherit the earth?" *Scientific American* 271(4):108–113 (October 1994).

157 Norbert Wiener, *The Human Use of Human Beings: Cybernetics and Society* (Houghton Mifflin, 1950).

158 Aldo Leopold, *Sand County Almanac* (Oxford University Press, 1949), p. 190.

158 Peter F. Drucker, "The age of social transformation," *The Atlantic Monthly* 274(5):53 (November 1994).

162 Paul Colinvaux, *The Fates of Nations* (Penguin, 1982).

163 Lewis Thomas, *The Medusa and the Snail* (Viking, 1979), p. 175.